Langenscheidt

Scientific English

für Mediziner und Naturwissenschaftler

Formulierungshilfen für wissenschaftliche Arbeiten, Publikationen und Vorträge

Zweite, erweiterte Auflage

von Dr. med. Christian Hrdina und Robert Hrdina

Langenscheidt

Berlin · München · Wien · Zürich · New York

Bibliografische Information der Deutschen Nationalbibliothek
Die Deutsche Nationalbibliothek verzeichnet diese Publikation in der Deutschen
Nationalbibliografie; detaillierte bibliografische Daten sind im Internet über
http://www.d-nb.de abrufbar.

2., erweiterte Auflage 2009
© 2009 Langenscheidt Fachverlag, ein Unternehmen der Langenscheidt KG,
Berlin und München
Satz: Claudia Wild, Stuttgart
Druck: CS-Druck, CornelsenStürtz, Berlin
Printed in Germany
ISBN 978-3-86117-309-0

09010

Inhaltsübersicht — Table of contents

Vorwort — 7

Benutzerhinweise — 9

I. Schriftliche Publikationen — Written publications — 13

A. Einführung — Introduction — 15

A 1.	Ziel der Studie	Aim of the study	15
A 2.	Gegenstand der Studie	Subject of the study	17
A 3.	Was ist neu?	What is new?	21

B. Material und Methodik — Materials and methods — 22

B 1.	Studienart und Methodik	Study type and methods	22
B 2.	Statistik	Statistical analysis	26
B 3.	Patientenkollektiv	Patient population	29
B 4.	Ethikkommission	Ethics committee	32

C. Ergebnisse — Results — 34

C 1.	Ergebnisse anführen	Listing results	34
C 2.	Mengenangaben (Grundlagen)	Quantities (Basics)	38
C 3.	Verweis auf Tabellen und Abbildungen	Links to tables and figures	42

D	**Diskussion**	**Discussion**	**45**
D 1.	Erwähnungen	How to mention	45
D 2.	Beschreibungen	How to describe	47
D 3.	Aufzählungen	How to enumerate	49
D 4.	Beispiele	How to give examples	51
D 5.	Betonungen und Hervorhebungen	How to emphasize	53
D 6.	Vergleiche und Gegenüberstellungen	How to compare and contrast	56
D 7.	Entwicklungen und Tendenzen	How to present development and change	60
D 8.	Wertung und Beurteilung	How to evaluate	62
D 9.	Vergleich mit Literatur	How to refer to the literature	64
D 9.1.	Ergebnisse anderer Studien	Results of other studies	64
D 9.2.	Gemeinsamkeiten	Common ground	69
D 9.3.	Unterschiede	Differences	71
D 10.	Beweisführung	How to argue	73
D 10.1.	Ursachenanalyse	Causal analysis	73
D 10.2.	Pro	How to argue for s.th.	77
D 10.3.	Contra	How to argue against s.th.	80
D 10.4.	Schlussfolgerungen	How to draw conclusions	82
D 11.	Zusammenhänge	How to explain relations	84
D 12.	Vermutungen	How to assume	88
D 13.	Meinungen	How to express opinions	90
D 14.	Mengenangaben (weiterführend)	How to use quantities (advanced)	92
D 15.	Zeitliche Angaben	How to integrate aspects of time	96
D 16.	Detailanalyse	How to analyse details	98
D 17.	Probleme und Limitierungen der Studie	How to point out problems and limitations	100
D 18.	Ausblick	Prospects	102

E	**Zusammenfassung**	**Summary**	**104**
F	**Danksagungen**	**Acknowledgements**	**106**
II.	**Vorträge**	**Oral presentation**	**109**
1.	Vorsitz und Moderation	Chairmanship	**111**
2.	Einleitung	Introduction	**117**
3.	Überleitungen	How to link up passages	**121**
4.	Dias, Folien und grafische Elemente	Slides, transparencies and graphics	**127**
5.	Hervorhebungen	How to emphasize	**133**
6.	Bezug nehmen auf andere Redner	Referring to other speakers	**136**
7.	Zusammenfassung / Schlusswort	Summary / Closing remarks	**137**
8.	Aufforderung zu Fragen	How to invite the audience to ask questions	**141**
9.	Antwort auf Fragen, Anmerkungen und Einwände	How to answer and retort	**145**
10.	Fragen und Kommentare anbringen	How to ask and comment	**153**
11.	Gemischtes & Nützliches	Miscellaneous & Useful	**157**

Appendix 1:   **Manuskripteinsendung / How to submit**   **163**

Appendix 2:   **Vergleich AE/BE / Comparison AE/BE**   **168**

Appendix 3:   **Ausflug ins Wirtschaftsenglisch / Business English Excursion**   **175**

Appendix 4: Kontakte knüpfen / Socialising 179

Appendix 5: E-Mails / Emails 184

Appendix 6: Glossar / Glossary 187

Bei der Neubearbeitung von *Scientific English* ergaben sich zum einen notwendige Ergänzungen in Form von eigenständigen Kapiteln (u. a. *Business English Excursion*; *Socialising*), zum anderen die Aufnahme weiterer nützlicher Phrasen und strukturierender Wendungen (sog. *signposts*) im mündlichen Teil. Authentische Sprachmodule wurden an geeigneter Stelle eingestreut, um die Aktualität und Authentizität von *Scientific English* angemessen zu verankern.
Die Autoren danken Sylvia Hrdina für das geübte Korrekturlesen. Unser besonderer Dank gilt dem Langenscheidt Fachverlag für die engagierte Umsetzung unseres Buchprojekts. Namentlich möchten wir ausdrücklich Frau Romina Brenna erwähnen für ihre tatkräftige und versierte Redaktionsarbeit.

Autoren und Verlag sind für sachdienliche Hinweise bzw. kritische Anmerkungen, die der weiteren Optimierung dieses Werkes dienen, dankbar. Diese sollten an den Langenscheidt Fachverlag, Postfach 40 11 20, D-80711 München gesendet werden.

Dr. med. Christian Hrdina
und Robert Hrdina

Vorwort zur 1. Auflage

Wer kennt das Problem nicht: Nach monate- oder gar jahrelanger Forschungsarbeit haben Sie vielversprechende Ergebnisse erzielt, die Sie möglichst schnell einem internationalen Fachpublikum zugänglich machen wollen. Schon lange wissen Sie, auf welchen Kongressen Sie Ihre Arbeit präsentieren möchten und welches Journal das geeignete Forum für eine Publikation wäre. Und schon lange ist Ihnen eines klar: Egal, was Sie mitzuteilen haben, es muss auf Englisch sein.
Mühsam und zeitraubend wird Satz für Satz konstruiert, immer wieder müssen Sie im Wörterbuch nachschlagen, und wenn endlich ein Absatz zu Papier gebracht ist, wirkt er doch streckenweise sprachlich unbeholfen und eintönig. Formulieren Sie Ihren Vortrag komplett aus und lernen ihn auswendig, oder sind Sie routiniert genug, um in freier Rede mit korrektem Englisch aufzutreten? Kündigen Sie Ihre Dias regelmäßig mit dem Ausspruch
Here you can see ... an? Bedienen Sie sich aus einem breiten Repertoire an englischen Ausdrucksweisen oder erschöpft sich Ihr angelerntes Englisch in festgefahrenen Redewendungen und rigiden Satzbauten?

Hier setzt unser Buch an mit dem Ziel, dem wissenschaftlichen Autor eine praktische und reichhaltige Formulierungshilfe zu bieten.
Auf der Basis mehrerer hundert medizinisch-naturwissenschaftlicher Artikel aus renommierten englischsprachigen Fachzeitschriften entstand dieses praxisorientierte Handbuch, das über 500 für das Scientific English essenzielle Begriffe und rund 900 universell anwendbare, authentische Satzbeispiele anschaulich präsentiert. Dabei werden auf dem internationalen wissenschaftlichen Publikationssektor unerfahrene und routinierte Fachautoren gleichermaßen angesprochen.

Der Aufbau von **Teil I Written publications – Schriftliche Publikationen** orientiert sich an der Standardgliederung eines wissenschaftlichen Artikels, so dass das Buch kontextbezogen während des gesamten Schreibvorgangs herangezogen werden kann. Es wurde versucht, typische und wiederkehrende Aspekte deskriptiven und argumentativen Schreibens möglichst umfassend abzubilden. Fundamentale Bereiche wie Aufzählungen und Vergleiche werden ebenso behandelt wie die Präsentation, Analyse, Abgrenzung und Diskussion eigener Forschungsergebnisse.

Analog werden im **Teil II Oral presentation – Vorträge** verschiedene situative Aspekte eines wissenschaftlichen Vortrags in gebrauchsfertigem Englisch dargeboten.

Im Anhang finden sich Formulierungsvorschläge für Anschreiben an Herausgeber wissenschaftlicher Fachzeitschriften im Rahmen der Manuskripteinsendung, ein Vergleich zwischen American English (AE) und British English (BE) sowie ein deutsch-englisches Glossar für Teil I.

Anders als zahllose Werke, die sich mit konzeptionellen und formalen Aspekten eines wissenschaftlichen Essays befassen, dient dieses Buch als unmittelbare Schreib- und Formulierungshilfe und verzichtet bewusst auf theoretische Abhandlungen über die Planung und Entstehung einer wissenschaftlichen Publikation. Dabei handelt es sich ausdrücklich nicht um ein Fachwörterbuch; Fachausdrücke aus der Medizin und naturwissenschaftlichen Disziplinen werden nur exemplarisch im Zusammenhang mit Beispielsätzen verwendet.

Wir wünschen allen Benutzern unbeschwertes und produktives Arbeiten mit unserem Buch, genügend Mut und Experimentierfreude im Umgang mit Scientific English und das nötige Glück auf dem Weg zur perfekten englischen Publikation.

Die Autoren danken Herrn Prof. Dr. med. Joachim Sciuk, Herrn Dr. Philip A. Luelsdorff und Herrn Dr. Manfred Eichhorn für die eingehende Begutachtung des Manuskripts und ihre fachlichen Ratschläge. Dank gilt ferner Gray Kochhar-Lindgren, PhD, für den langjährigen linguistischen Gedankenaustausch.

Christian Hrdina, Robert Hrdina

Scientific English für Mediziner und Naturwissenschaftler gliedert sich in **Teil I Written publications – Schriftliche Publikationen** und **Teil II Oral presentation – Vorträge.**

Der Aufbau von Teil I folgt der Standardgliederung eines medizinisch-naturwissenschaftlichen Artikels, um ein möglichst zeitsparendes, kontextbezogenes Nachschlagen benötigter Begriffe zu ermöglichen.

Am Beginn jedes Kapitels wird das jeweilige Basisvokabular dargeboten (**blaue Schrift**). Im Anschluss folgen weiterführende Begriffe (Aufbauvokabular; **schwarze Schrift**) mit Variationen des Basisvokabulars, sowie zahlreiche englische Satzbeispiele zu den verwendeten Begriffen (siehe Schema).

Diese authentischen Beispielsätze können unmittelbar in die eigene wissenschaftliche Arbeit übernommen und thematisch adaptiert werden.

Längere Abschnitte mit Aufbauvokabular und Satzbeispielen gliedern sich in übersichtliche Einheiten, die den Erfordernissen des jeweiligen Kapitels angepasst sind (z. B. Zusammenfassung von Synonymen, Sortierung nach auf- bzw. absteigenden Kriterien, Gruppierung von Gegensatzpaaren etc.).

Werden mehrere englische Begriffe mit gleichlautender deutscher Übersetzung dargeboten, so sind diese synonym verwendbar. Im Falle semantischer Unterschiede zwischen solchen Vokabeln wird explizit darauf hingewiesen.

Sie werden einigen Vokabeln mehrfach begegnen, da diese für verschiedene Kapitel gleichermaßen von Relevanz sind.

In Teil II werden – sortiert nach unterschiedlichen Sprechsituationen – mehr als 600 universell verwendbare Formulierungen für wissenschaftliche Vorträge in englischer Sprache dargeboten. Hierbei wurde auf eine separate Vokabelliste bewusst verzichtet.

Auf Unterschiede im British English (BE) und American English (AE) wird an geeigneter Stelle hingewiesen. Teil II folgt durchweg der britischen Schreibweise, ebenso wie das deutsch-englische Glossar.

9

Englisches **Basisvokabular** für das jeweilige Kapitel

A 1. Ziel der Studie / Aim of the study

Basisvokabular

aim	Ziel
to aim	beabsichtigen
goal	Ziel
objective	Ziel
intent	Absicht
purpose	Zweck
focus	Schwerpunkt, Hauptaugenmerk

Rechte Spalte:
Deutsche Übersetzungen

Aufbauvokabular und Satzbeispiele

aim	The **aim** of this study was to evaluate perioperative morbidity of laparoscopic cholecystectomy.	Ziel
to aim	We **aimed** to …	beabsichtigen
goal	The **goal** of this study was to … The primary **goal** of the study was to …	Ziel
objective	The **objective** of this study is to determine whether … Our main **objective** was to determine whether …	Ziel
intent	The **intent** was to …	Absicht
purpose	The **purpose** of this article is to review … The **purpose** of this study wa...	Zweck

Variationen des **Basisvokabulars +** **Aufbauvokabular**

Mittlere Spalte:
„Gebrauchsfertige" englische Beispielsätze

AE	American English (amerikanisches Englisch)
BE	British English (britisches Englisch)
d. h.	das heißt
e.g.	exempli gratia, for example (zum Beispiel)
etw.	etwas
i. d. R.	in der Regel
i.e.	id est, that is (das heißt)
i. S. v.	im Sinne von
jmdm.	jemandem
jmdn.	jemanden
o. g.	oben genannt
s.b.	somebody (jemand)
s.o.	someone (jemand)
s.th.	something (etwas)
u. a.	und andere, unter anderem
v. a.	vor allem
z. B.	zum Beispiel
*	bezeichnet im Appendix 2 einen stilistisch bzw. grammatikalisch untragbaren Satz
/	etw. genauer/detailliert erläutern = etw. genauer erläutern oder etw. detailliert erläutern
( )	(heraus)finden = finden oder herausfinden

Wichtiger Hinweis:

Die beschriebenen naturwissenschaftlichen und medizirischen Begebenheiten und Zahlenangaben stellen nicht in allen Fällen reelle Tatsachen dar und dienen nur zur Veranschaulichung eines sprachlichen Sachverhalts. Entsprechende Angaben können nicht als Grundlage für wissenschaftliche und medizinische Arbeit jeglicher Art herangezogen werden.
Verwendete Personen- und Institutsnamen sowie Zeitschriftentitel sind frei erfunden und besitzen lediglich Beispielcharakter. Jegliche Ähnlichkeit mit real existierenden Personen, Instituten und Medien ist rein zufällig.

Schriftliche Publikationen
Written publications

A   Einführung / Introduction

A 1. Ziel der Studie / Aim of the study

Basisvokabular

aim	Z el
to aim	beabsichtigen
goal	Z el
objective	Z el
intent	Absicht
purpose	Zweck
focus	Schwerpunkt, Hauptaugenmerk

Aufbauvokabular und Satzbeispiele

aim	The **aim** of this study was to evaluate perioperative morbidity of laparc-scopic cholecystectomy.	Ziel
to aim	We **aimed** to …	beabsichtigen
goal	The **goal** of this study was to .. The primary **goal** of the study was to …	Ziel
objective	The **objective** of this study is to determine whether … Our main **objective** was to determine whether …	Ziel
intent	The **intent** was to …	Absicht

I. A 1. Ziel der Studie

purpose	The **purpose** of this article is to review …	Zweck
	The **purpose** of this study was to establish whether …	
	The **purpose** of the study was to evaluate the safety of these neuro-protective drugs.	
focus	The **focus** of this article is …	Schwerpunkt, Hauptaugenmerk
to be intended to	The report **is intended to** summarize the …	beabsichtigen
in order to	This prospective study was conducted **in order to** evaluate the safety of the new procedure.	um zu
to set out to	We **set out to** investigate various aspects of …	beabsichtigen
to attempt	We have **attempted** to describe a range of …	versuchen
target group	Our **target group** is best defined as follows: …	Zielgruppe
priority	Our first **priority** was to treat the genetic manipulation of crops as an issue of great current interest and controversy.	Vorrang, Priorität
	… has not been one of our **priorities**.	
	We had to accord **priority** to this **goal**.	

A 2. Gegenstand der Studie / Subject of the study

Basisvokabular

study	Studie
survey	Erhebung, Übersicht, Überblick
review	Übersichtsarbeit
article	Artikel
report	Bericht
essay	Essay, Fachaufsatz
analysis	Analyse
work	Arbeit
investigation	Untersuchung
research	Forschung

Aufbauvokabular und Satzbeispiele

to perform (a study)	This **study** was **performed** in order to measure the increase in atmospheric carbon dioxide concentration.	(eine Studie) durchführen
to conduct (a study)	The Association of Abdominal Surgeons **conducted** a prospective **study** of 1,518 patients who underwent gastrectomy. Here we **conduct** an extensive **investigation** of …	(eine Studie) durchführen
survey	A national **survey** was therefore **conducted** to broadly estimate the frequency of major complications associated with this technique. This **survey** was **conducted** between January 2001 and June 2002.	Erhebung, Übersicht, Überblick

17

I. A 2. Gegenstand der Studie

	A **survey** published in last month's issue of *The Lancet* and **conducted** by Hamilton Polls Int., reveals most striking figures in respect of …	
to present review	This **review presents** … The authors **present** the potential of … Here we **present** new evidence that …	präsentieren, vorstellen Übersichtsarbeit
to address s.th.	This **study addresses** the question in a more structured way. This **study addresses** the issue of angioplasty in an unconventional way.	etw. ansprechen
to describe article	In this **article** we **describe** …	beschreiben Artikel
report	This **report describes** the results of …	Bericht
to illustrate	This pictorial **essay describes** and **illustrates** heat flux anomalies in Antarctica over the past ten years.	illustrieren, veranschauli-chen
to review s.th.	This **article reviews** the aetiologies and imaging findings of acute mesenteric ischemia. In this **article**, the CT findings of acute mesenteric ischemia are **reviewed**.	einen Überblick geben über etw.
to investigate analysis	The current **analysis investigated** the hypothesis that …	untersuchen Analyse
essay	In this **essay**, we have tried to **investigate** …	Essay, Fachaufsatz
to examine work	Our **work examines** …	untersuchen Arbeit

to explore	Throughout this **analysis** we **explore** the structure of bacterial outer membrane lipoproteins.	erforschen, untersuchen
to test	The purpose of the **study** was to **test** the clinical feasibility and utility of a new scanning protocol.	testen, prüfen
to determine	This **study** was performed to **determine** differences in electron dynamics. A portion of this **study** was dedicated to **determining** whether any time difference was noticeable between the two technologies.	feststellen, bestimmen
to evaluate **investigation**	In our **investigation**, we **evaluated** …	einschätzen, beurteilen, bewerten Untersuchung
to assess	In our **research**, we **assessed** …	einschätzen, beurteilen, bewerten
		INFO: **To evaluate** *und* **to assess** *werden hier synonym gebraucht. Bei der Auswertung von Ergebnissen wird nur* **to evaluate results** *verwendet.*
research		Forschung
question of interest	Yet another **question of interest** for us was …	interessante Fragestellung
concern	Of additional **concern** has been the value of satellite magnetic data.	Belang
to concern oneself with s.th.	In this **study**, **we concerned ourselves with** the impact that this method had on climate prediction.	sich mit etw. befassen

I. A 2. Gegenstand der Studie

to offer insight into s.th.	This **investigation** **offers insight into** …	Einblick in etw. gewähren
to compare s.th. with s.th.	This **investigation** **compared** … **with** …	etw. mit etw. vergleichen
to settle a question	This **study** **settles the** important **question** of whether laser dissection or cautery is better for the removal of the gall bladder from the hepatic bed.	eine Frage (eindeutig/ endgültig) beantworten

Basisvokabular

new	neu
novel	neuartig

Aufbauvokabular und Satzbeispiele

new	What is **new** is …	neu
	We report a **new** method of …	
	Here we propose a **new** technique …	
	We have developed a **new** technology to assess …	
	Here we present **new** evidence that …	
novel	We report a **novel** process of …	neuartig
for the first time	Here we report/show/demonstrate/ present **for the first time** that …	zum ersten Mal, erstmalig
	The observation reported here provides **for the first time** key insight into …	
	For the first time, we believe (to be able) to shed light on …	
	Here we describe a hitherto ignored phenomenon, namely …	
	Unlike many of our predecessors, we …	**INFO:** *Die nebenstehenden Beispielsätze beinhalten kein neues Vokabular. Sie stellen lediglich weitere themenbezogene Formulierungsmöglichkeiten dar.*
	Our results challenge previous claims that …	
	Altogether, these results bring **new** constraints to models for …	
	So far, this procedure has been limited to …	
	Here we present a model that goes much further.	

B 1. Studienart und Methodik / Study type and methods

Basisvokabular

data	Daten
questionnaire	Fragebogen
respondent	Befragte(r)
rate of return	Rücklaufquote
response rate	Antwortrate
study protocol	Studienprotokoll
method	Methode
supplementary information	(Informations-)Beilage
follow-up	Follow-Up, Nachbeobachtung
period	Zeitraum

Aufbauvokabular und Satzbeispiele

data

Data was summarized with regard to overall morbidity, mortality, length of hospital stay, and duration of postoperative recovery.

The **data** summarized in this review represent the initial experience with genomic sequencing.

According to Cli-Mac Research Solutions there are no comprehensive **data** on growth and reproduction.

Daten

INFO: *Im Englischen kann* **data** *sowohl im Singular als auch im Plural verwendet werden. Ursprünglich fand sich der Singulargebrauch v. a. im AE. Einige Autoren im wissenschaftlichen Bereich beharren auf dem strikten Pluralgebrauch, so wird beispielsweise in Handblättern der naturwis-*

	senschaftlichen Fakultäten der britischen University of Hull **data** *konsequent in der Pluralform verwendet. Beide Formen finden sich in der Literatur jedoch gleichsam.*	
to express data	All **data** are **expressed** as mean values ±1 standard deviation.	Daten angeben
available	Reliable **data** was **available** for 162 probes.	verfügbar
questionnaire	The **questionnaire** was structured to focus on major procedure-related injuries. We have designed the **questionnaire** as follows: …	Fragebogen
respondent	A total of 413 **respondents** have submitted valuable data.	Befragte(r)
rate of return	They provided an adequate **rate of return**.	Rücklaufquote
response rate	The **response rate** was 68%.	Antwortrate
to provide	1,200 institutions **provided** specific numerical **data**.	liefern
to submit	A total of 45 institutions **submitted** prospective **data** from September 1990 to August 1992.	zur Verfügung stellen, einreichen
to query	Mortality was not specifically **queried**.	erfragen
study protocol	The **study protocol** included the acquisition of 2-dimensional echocardiography to evaluate regional wall motion.	Studienprotokoll

I. B 1. Studienart und Methodik

method	We have applied the subsequent **methods**: …	Methode
to retrieve	All CT scans of the upper cervical region performed between April and November 1999 were **retrieved** for study.	heranziehen
to record	The Swedish surgical registry prospectively **recorded** 1,164 appendectomies during the years 1991-1993.	verzeichnen, aufzeichnen
to screen (for)	Patients were **screened for** the presence of free intraperitoneal gas.	bezüglich etw. untersuchen, auf etw. hin untersuchen
to monitor	Our aim was to **monitor** hypocentral stresses in the earthquake.	beobachten, aufzeichnen
to measure	Leukocyte counts were **measured** in the same week that the scintigraphy was performed.	messen
supplementary information	Protein purification is described in the **Supplementary Information**. Proteins were incubated for 30 minutes as recommended by … (see **Supplementary Information**). For further details of the incubation procedure see **Supplementary Information**.	(Informations-)Beilage **INFO: Supplementary Information** *wird dann groß geschrieben, wenn diese Journalbeilage explizit so betitelt ist.*
follow-up	On **follow-up** at 6 mo, 3 patients had severe restenosis of the infarct-related vessel. **Follow-up** was available for 51 of these 87 patients.	Follow-Up, Nachbeobachtung
to follow s.th. up	Our plan is to **follow** this population **up** for a several-year period.	etw. nachbeobachten
period	This study was conducted over a several-year **period**.	Zeitraum

to collect data about s.th.	We **collected** data **about** marine mammal mortality in the Baltic Sea. Data was **collected** prospectively.	über etw. Daten erheben
to gather information about s.th.	The main focus of this study was to **gather information about** the procedure-related morbidity after endoscopic sphincterotomy.	über etw. Informationen gewinnen
to glean s.th.	These facts have been **gleaned** following a thorough analysis of old hospital files.	herausfinden, (mühsam) in Erfahrung bringen
to gain knowledge of s.th.	The objective has been to **gain knowledge of** the mechanisms …	über etw. Kenntnis erlangen
to obtain s.th.	We have **obtained** data about 1,245 consecutive cases.	etw. erhalten, gewinnen

B 2. Statistik / Statistical analysis

Basisvokabular

significance	Signifikanz
significant	signifikant
to test	testen
to calculate	berechnen
to analyse (BE) to analyze (AE)	analysieren
to evaluate	einschätzen, beurteilen, bewerten
to assess	einschätzen, beurteilen, bewerten
to determine	bestimmen
to compare	vergleichen
to examine	untersuchen

Aufbauvokabular und Satzbeispiele

significant	A probability P value of less than 0.05 was considered **significant**. $P < 0.05$ was considered to indicate a statistically **significant** difference. These differences were not statistically **significant**. The reduction in the conversion rate between the two laparoscopic groups from 5.2 to 1.8% was statistically **significant**.	signifikant
significance	The hypothesis that … was examined by **using** the χ^2-test for trend, with **significance** assigned at the 5% level.	Signifikanz

	Error probabilities below 0.05 were accepted to denote statistical **significance**.	
to test	Waste-water was **tested** for …	testen
to carry out a test	**Tests** have been **carried out** to determine the speed of migration.	einen Test durchführen
to use (a test) **to calculate**	The χ^2-test was **used** to **calculate** the difference …	(einen Test) verwenden berechnen
to analyse (BE) **to analyze** (AE)	The χ^2-test was **used** to **analyse** (BE)/**analyze** (AE) the difference …	analysieren
to test	The χ^2-test was **used** to **test** the difference …	testen
to evaluate	The χ^2-test was **used** to **evaluate** the difference in sensitivity.	einschätzen, beurteilen, bewerten
to assess	The χ^2-test was **used** to **assess** the difference …	einschätzen, beurteilen, bewerten
		INFO: To evaluate *und* **to assess** *werden hier synonym gebraucht. Bei der Auswertung von Ergebnissen wird nur* **to evaluate results** *verwendet.*
assessment	Differences in the **assessment** of the TNM-System stage between the different imaging procedures were **tested** for **significance** by McNemar's test.	Beurteilung, Bemessung
to determine	The χ^2-test was **used** to **determine** the difference …	bestimmen
to perform (a test)	The χ^2-test was **performed** to **evaluate** the difference …	(einen Test) durchführen

I. B 2. Statistik

to compare	The χ^2-test was **performed** to **compare** the sensitivity of …	vergleichen
to employ (a test)	We **employed** the χ^2-test to **analyse** *(BE)*/**analyze** *(AE)* whether …	(einen Test) anwenden
to examine	The hypothesis that … was **examined** by **using** the χ^2-test statistic.	untersuchen
to perform	Analysis was **performed** (by) using *Softwarename (Softwarefirma, Firmensitz)*. Statistical calculations were **performed** (by) using a statistical software package *(Softwarename 1 und Softwarename 2, Softwarefirma, Firmensitz)*. All statistical analyses described above were **performed** (by) using the software program *Softwarename (Softwarefirma, Firmensitz)*.	durchführen
to process	All data were **processed** using *Softwarename (Softwarefirma, Firmensitz)*.	verarbeiten

B 3. Patientenkollektiv / Patient population

Basisvokabular

inclusion	Einschluss
exclusion	Ausschluss
patient population	Patientenpopulation, Patientenkollektiv
sample	Stichprobe
cohort	Kohorte, Reihe (von Probanden)
series	Reihe, Serie
subject	Gegenstand, Thema *hier*: Person
individuals	Individuen

Aufbauvokabular und Satzbeispiele

inclusion criterion **exclusion criterion**	**Inclusion** and **exclusion** **criteria** were defined by an expert panel.	Einschlusskriterium Ausschlusskriterium
sample	Small **sample** size resulted from strict **exclusion** **criteria**. The patient **sample included** 28 men and 97 women.	Stichprobe
to include	The study **included** 108 patients. 58 patients were **included**.	einschließen
patient population	The **patient population included** 54 consecutive patients.	Patientenpopulation, Patientenkollektiv
to exclude	Patients were **excluded** in the case of …	ausschließen

I. B 3. Patientenkollektiv

to comprise	The series **comprised** two groups of patients who …	einschließen
to consist of	The **patient population** **consisted of** 108 patients with …	sich zusammensetzen aus
to enlist	Five consecutive patients were **enlisted** from the acute trauma service.	einschließen, rekrutieren
to enrol **series**	A **series** of 187 patients was **enrolled**.	einschließen, rekrutieren Reihe, Serie
to select	For the study, 46 patients were **selected**.	auswählen
patient selection	**Patient selection** in this retrospective analysis was biased/biassed.	Patientenauswahl **INFO:** *Beide Schreibweisen sind gebräuchlich.*
to recruit	The patients **recruited** for this study showed …	rekrutieren
cohort	A **cohort** of 108 patients was **recruited**.	Kohorte, Reihe (von Probanden)
recruitment criteria	**Recruitment criteria** were: …	Auswahlkriterien
to participate (in s.th.)	Six healthy male volunteers **participated in** this study.	(an etw.) teilnehmen
to take part (in s.th.)	46 patients with osteoarthritis **took part in** this investigation.	(an etw.) teilnehmen
to group	The **series** were **grouped** into either single-centre or multicentre *(BE)*/ multicenter *(AE)* reviews. We **grouped** patients with unilateral renal artery stenosis of 50–75% and patients with unilateral renal artery stenosis greater than 75%.	gruppieren; in Kategorien einteilen

group **subgroup**	Two **groups** of patients were formed and divided into five **subgroups** each.	Gruppe Untergruppe
to randomise *(BE)* **to randomize** *(AE)* **subject**	40 **subjects** were **randomised** *(BE)*/ **randomized** *(AE)* to group A and 40 to group B.	randomisiert zuteilen Person
to classify (as)	The patient was **classified as** severely injured if …	klassifizieren, einstufen (als)
to define (as)	Three groups of patients were **defined**: …	definieren (als)
age	Mean patient **age** was 61 years (range 21–88 years). The **age** of the patients ranged from 8 to 98 years. The patients averaged 47 years of **age**.	Alter
total **in total**	The **series** included a **total** of 12,397 patients. Of this **total**, 758 patients were treated at academic hospitals and 504 at private institutions. **In total**, 342 blood samples were tested for traces of …	Gesamtheit, Gesamtzahl insgesamt
overall **individuals**	**Overall**, 700 **subjects** were tested for symptoms of … An **overall** of 500 **individuals** took **part in** …	insgesamt, Gesamtheit, Gesamtzahl Individuen

B 4. Ethikkommission / Ethics committee

Basisvokabular

ethics committee	Ethikkommission
approval	Zustimmung
informed consent	aufgeklärtes Einverständnis

Aufbauvokabular und Satzbeispiele

to approve	The investigational review board **approved** the study.	zustimmen (*i. S. v.* absegnen, genehmigen)
	The study was **approved** by the local institutional review board.	**INFO:** *Im Zusammenhang mit einem Genehmigungsverfahren sollte* **to approve s.th.** *verwendet werden. Das umgangssprachlich gelegentlich synonym gebrauchte* **to approve of s.th.** *bedeutet soviel wie „Gefallen finden an etw."und zieht nicht notwendigerweise die offizielle Erteilung einer Studiengenehmigung nach sich.*
	The study has been **approved** by the university ethics committee and federal authorities.	
informed consent	All candidates gave written **informed consent**, and the study was **approved** by the institutional review board.	aufgeklärtes Einverständnis
	In patients under the age of 18, **informed consent** was also obtained from the parents.	
	This study was **approved** by the committee on human research. Written **informed consent** was not required.	

ethics committee approval	**Informed consent** and **ethics committee approval** <u>was</u> obtained.	Ethikkommission Zustimmung (*i. S. v.* Absegnung, Genehmigung)
		INFO: *Beide Formen (Singular/Plural) sind gebräuchlich. Bevorzugt sollte* **were** *verwendet werden.*
	Institutional review board **approval** and **informed** patient **consent** <u>were</u> obtained.	
to endorse	The **ethics committee endorsed** the study design prior to patient acquisition.	zustimmen, gutheißen
		INFO: *Synonym zu* **to approve**
	The **ethics committee** of our institution **endorsed** the study protocol. The protocol was **endorsed** by the **ethics committee** of our institution and each subject gave **informed** written **consent**.	
to waive	**Informed consent** was **waived**.	auf etw. verzichten
exemption (from)	This investigation met the criteria for an **exemption from** institutional review board **approval**.	Ausnahme (von), Freistellung (von)
to require	Neither institutional board **approval** nor **informed consent** were **required**.	erfordern

C 1. Ergebnisse anführen / Listing results

Basisvokabular

result	Resultat, Ergebnis
finding	Ergebnis, Schluss
outcome	Ergebnis
to find	(heraus)finden, zu einem Ergebnis kommen
to observe	beobachten
to encounter s.th.	etw. begegnen, auftreten (etw. tritt auf)
rate	Häufigkeit, Rate
frequency	Häufigkeit
incidence	Inzidenz
gamut	Bandbreite, Spektrum
scale	Bandbreite, Spektrum
to range from ... to ...	von ... bis ... reichen
to vary from ... to ...	von ... bis ... variieren

Aufbauvokabular und Satzbeispiele

result	Our study has yielded the following **results**: …	Resultat, Ergebnis
finding	The main **finding** of this study is that 98% of the patient population showed the same symptoms after succinylcholine had been administered.	Ergebnis, Schluss

	We have **encountered** contradictory **findings**.	
outcome	All the applied pharmaceuticals led to the same **outcome**.	Ergebnis
to find	We **found** abnormal prior strains in more than 29% of the samples. The highest endothelin-1 concentrations were **found** in the four patients with injury-severity scores of more than 40. The remaining 5 patients were **found** to have gallstones.	(heraus)finden, zu einem Ergebnis kommen
to observe	Instantaneous vaporization was **observed** in 8 of 63 different settings.	beobachten
to encounter s.th.	Amyloid fibrils were **encountered** in 109 probes.	etw. begegnen, auftreten (etw. tritt auf)
to see **to be seen**	Septic shock was **seen** in 14 patients.	beobachten auftreten
to come across s.th.	When analysing the final data, we **came across** three major aberrations.	auf etw. stoßen, etw. begegnen
to detect	We **detected** a significant deviation from the mean value.	feststellen, entdecken
to identify	Significant deviations were **identified** in 1,586 probes.	feststellen
to reveal	Overall, 55 gastroduodenal perforations were **revealed**.	feststellen, sich zeigen
to indicate	These data **indicate** aberrant stages of protein synthesis.	anzeigen, hinweisen (auf), darauf hindeuten
to be present	Wound infections **were present** in more than one third of all patients.	auftreten

I. C 1. Ergebnisse anführen

to occur	All 15 deaths **occurred** among the 2,360 patients older than 65 years. This phenomenon **occurred** in 0.14%.	auftreten
occurrence	Specific queries included the **frequency** of injury to the aorta and the **occurrence** of any delayed complications.	das Auftreten
evidence of s.th.	There was **evidence of** biotic loss in the ecosystem observed.	Nachweis von etw.
rate	The mean **rate** of vessel injury was 0.6%. The technique is associated with low **rates** of morbidity and mortality.	Häufigkeit, Rate
frequency	Intracranial bleeding occurred with a **frequency** of 14%.	Häufigkeit
incidence	Patients treated for acute cholecystitis had an **incidence** of postoperative complications of 17.1%. The **incidence** of bile duct injury in the first 90 patients was 2.2%, as compared with 0.1% for subsequent patients.	Inzidenz
to stand at	The death **rate** in this unselected series **stands at** 0.5%.	sich belaufen auf
to represent	This **represents** a mortality **rate** of 0.6% in this group.	darstellen, entsprechen
gamut	The reported injuries ran the whole **gamut** of severe traumatic lesions.	Bandbreite, Spektrum
scale	The **scale** of antibiotics **ranged from** … **to** …	Bandbreite, Spektrum
to range from … to …	Mortality **rates ranged from** 0.5% **to** 1.0%. Mortality from this disorder remains high, **ranging from** 70% **to** 90%.	von … bis … reichen

to vary from ... to ...	Contemporary **rates** of contamination **vary from** 0% **to** 0.4% and are often cited at 0.1% to 0.25%. The sensitivity **varied from** 62% **to** 44%.	von ... bis ... variieren
respectively	The **incidence** of major bile duct injury, vessel injury and overall morbidity was 0.3%, 0.4% and 4% **respectively**.	beziehungsweise

Basisvokabular

many	viele
a number of	eine Reihe (von)
a score of	eine Reihe (von)
some	manche
a few	ein paar, einige
few	wenige
little	wenig (bei nicht zählbaren Dingen)
high	hoch
low	niedrig
rate	Rate
percentage	Prozentsatz, prozentualer Anteil
proportion	Anteil, Verhältnis
part	Teil
partial(ly)	teilweise
fraction	Bruchteil
half of	die Hälfte von
one third/quarter of	ein Drittel/Viertel von
majority	Mehrheit
minority	Minderheit
all (of)	alle, alles

none (of)	niemand, nichts
total	gesamt, komplett, Gesamtheit
in total	zusammen, alles in allem
overall	insgesamt Gesamt…

Aufbauvokabular und Satzbeispiele

many	**Many** aspects of bacterial fermentation deserve further investigation.	viele
a number of	**A number of** previous studies have used ventilation scans as a clinical tool.	eine Reihe (von)
a score of	**A score of** surveys have reported …	eine Reihe (von)
some	**Some** experts claim that …	manche
a few	We could isolate only **a few** samples of …	ein paar, einige
few	**Few** institutions have so far adopted the new technique.	wenige
little	Technical aspects were of **little** interest to us.	wenig *(bei nicht zählbaren Dingen)*
high	The **high** number of … is explained by …	hoch
low	Total organic carbon was relatively **low**.	niedrig
	20% of the prion strains showed signs of … **In 20% of** the events, we observed signs of … **In** 97 **of** the 118 cases, .. **Of** the 25 patients studied, 4 had a history of previous myocardial infarction.	**INFO**: *Die nebenstehenden Beispielsätze beinhalten kein neues Vokabular. Sie stellen lediglich weitere themenbezogene Formulierungsmöglichkeiten dar.*

I. C 2. Mengenangaben (Grundlagen)

rate	The method is generally associated with a low **rate** of postoperative morbidity.	Rate
percentage	A **high percentage** of these complications can be attributed to …	Prozentsatz, prozentualer Anteil
proportion	A significantly **lower proportion** of dolphins showed signs of brevetoxin inhalation in group 1 than in group 2.	Anteil, Verhältnis
part	Intraoperative bleeding accounted for the smallest **part** of all complications.	Teil
partial(ly)	The amino-terminal region is **partially** responsible for converting soluble protein into amyloid fibres *(BE)*/fibers *(AE)*.	teilweise
fraction	A tiny **fraction** of the overall population, namely 0.3%, showed minor complications.	Bruchteil
half of	More than **half of** the patient population suffered from severe abdominal injury.	die Hälfte von
one third of	Nonetheless, more than **one third of** the reported deaths were attributable to a technical complication.	ein Drittel von
majority	The **majority** of wildlife species in Bolivia show/shows …	Mehrheit
minority	Only a **minority** of the analysed *(BE)*/ analyzed *(AE)* samples was/were …	Minderheit

> **INFO: Majority/minority** *kann sowohl im Singular als auch im Plural gebraucht werden.*

40

all (of)	**All** samples were evaluated for … **All of** the molecules had …	alle, alles
none (of)	**None of** the mycoparasites had …	niemand, nichts
total	A **total** of 7,604 splenectomies was reported.	gesamt, komplett, Gesamtheit
in total	**In total**, 57 large vessels were injured.	zusammen, alles in allem
overall	**Overall**, the most common complication was … **Overall**, 55 gastroduodenal perforations were revealed. They described an **overall** morbidity rate of 4.5%.	insgesamt, Gesamt…

C 3. Verweis auf Tabellen und Abbildungen / Links to tables and figures

Basisvokabular

table	Tabelle
figure	Abbildung
diagram	Diagramm
chart	Schaubild, Tabelle, Diagramm
graph	Schaubild, Diagramm Kurve, Funktion

INFO: Die Beispielsätze dieses Kapitels sind prinzipiell auf jede der o.g. Basisvokabeln anwendbar.

Aufbauvokabular und Satzbeispiele

table	Between 1991 and 1998 complication rates decreased from 8.3 to 4.1% (**Table** 5).	Tabelle
to show	**Table** 2 **shows** …	zeigen
bullet point	There are seven **bullet points** under the first header. You find these **bullet points** under the heading "Absorbance".	Stichpunkt, Aufzählungspunkt
figure	The field intensity variations are **shown** in **Figure** 4. **Figure** 8 **shows** the same data as **Figure** 6, but with a different choice of axis scale. The relationship of perfusion distribution to lung water distribution is **shown** in **Figure** 7 by combining the data from **Figures** 4 and 6.	Abbildung

to list	Table 2 lists … Brevetoxin concentrations in sea-grass are **listed** in Table 1.	auflisten
to give	Table 5 **gives** the most frequent alternative diagnoses encountered. Table 5 **gives** the estimated sensitivities of each imaging technique. The estimates of site temperature changes are **given** in Tables 2 and 3.	zeigen, darbieten
to present	Table 3 **presents** … Results of kinetic analysis are **presented** in Table 1.	präsentieren, zeigen
to report	Clinical, pathological and imaging data are **reported** in Table 1.	darlegen
to indicate	The types of intravenous contrast media used are **indicated** in Table 4.	aufzeigen
to demonstrate	Figure 5 **demonstrates** a focus of increased activity in the inferior pole of the right thyroid lobe.	demonstrieren, zeigen
to highlight diagram	Diagram 4 **highlights** the recent development in …	hervorheben, verdeutlichen Diagramm
chart	Chart 4 **gives** the best-fit quadratic (parabola).	Schaubild, Tabelle, Diagramm **INFO:** **Chart** *ist ein universell verwendbarer Begriff für jegliche Art von visuellem Schaubild.*
flow chart	This **flow chart** should help you (to) decide whether or not to use a best-fit line or a best-fit curve.	Flussdiagramm

I. C 3. Verweis auf Tabellen und Abbildungen

pie chart	The caption for the following **pie chart** reads "Factors in Anthropogenic Global Warming".	Kreisdiagramm, Torten-diagramm
bar chart	The title of this **bar chart** incidentally is the same as that of **Table** 6.	Balkendiagramm
graph	When drawing two different sets of data on the same page with the same set of axes, the points for each individual **graph** should be distinguished by using a different symbol.	Schaubild, Diagramm Kurve, Funktion
scatter plot	**Scatter plots** in the natural sciences are also known as x-y plots.	Streudiagramm
to reflect	This development is **reflected** in **Table** 2.	widerspiegeln
to summarize	**Table** 2 **summarizes** the differences in protein coding genes between the two parasites. **Table** 1 and 2 **summarize** … Individual patient data are **summarized** in Table 1.	zusammenfassen
to combine	**Table** 4 **combines** the findings of the two studies.	zusammenfügen
to compare	**Figure** 2 **compares** bacterial growth in various soil types.	vergleichen

D 1. Erwähnungen / How to mention

Basisvokabular

to name	nennen, anführen
to mention	erwähnen bemerken
to observe	beobachten, feststellen
to perceive	bemerken, wahrnehmen
to encounter s.th.	etw. begegnen, auftreten (etw. tritt auf)
to detect	entdecken, feststellen
to report	berichten, erwähnen
to reveal	aufdecken, feststellen
to disclose	aufdecken, bekannt machen

Aufbauvokabular und Satzbeispiele

to name	Of the many different aspects associated with the use of sedatives, we would like to **name** the following: …	nennen, anführen
to mention	In this context, one has to **mention** the extraordinary impact of the new technique on patients' acceptance. The significantly shorter incubation time should also be **mentioned** here.	erwähnen, bemerken
to observe	We have **observed** a significant decrease of non-surgical complications like thrombosis, pneumonia or myocardial infarction. This was **observed** despite the fact that …	beobachten, feststellen

45

I. D 1. Erwähnungen

to perceive	It has been **perceived** that all tested proteins showed a rapid increase in fluorescence.	bemerken, wahrnehmen
to encounter s.th.	Bowel injuries were **encountered** in 109 patients.	etw. begegnen, auftreten (etw. tritt auf)
to detect	We have **detected** symptoms of inflammation in 29 of 413 patients.	entdecken, feststellen
to report	We **report** the results of a multicentre (BE)/multicenter (AE) survey among German university hospitals between 1991 and 1998.	berichten, erwähnen
to reveal	A closer examination **revealed** that these amide stacks stabilize the macromolecular aggregates.	aufdecken, feststellen
to disclose	The prospective type of registration tends to **disclose** minor faults and omit major ones.	aufdecken, bekannt machen
to consider	**Considering** the large and widely distributed nature of the sample, these results provide … Other issues worth **considering** are …	bedenken, erwägen
to take into consideration	The staggering acceptance of this new treatment by the patient population must also be **taken into consideration**.	in Erwägung ziehen, in Betracht ziehen
to take into account	**Taking** this **into account**, the total scanning time may be considered to be 5 min.	in Erwägung ziehen, in Betracht ziehen, mit einbeziehen
to acknowledge	One should **acknowledge** the fact that …	bedenken, anerkennen

Basisvokabular

to describe	beschreiben
to illustrate	illustrieren, verdeutlichen
to delineate	schildern, plakativ darstellen
to depict	darstellen
to scrutinize	unter die Lupe nehmen
to specify	verdeutlichen

Aufbauvokabular und Satzbeispiele

to describe	This pictorial essay **describes** the use of multislice helical CT. This list of results helps to **describe** a textbook pregnancy.	beschreiben
to illustrate	These studies **illustrate** the effectiveness of the novel method for monitoring breast cancer patients for recurrent disease.	illustrieren, verdeutlichen
to delineate	The following paragraph **delineates** in great detail the different steps of the procedure.	schildern, plakativ darstellen
to depict	Figure 7 **depicts** the effects of the new agent on blood pressure and heart rate. The negative effect of hypobaric hypoxia on lowlanders at high altitude has long been known and variously been **depicted** by numerous scientists worldwide.	darstellen

I. D 2. Beschreibungen

| to scrutinize | Smith et al. **scrutinized** the correlation between these two parameters in 1994. | unter die Lupe nehmen |
| to specify | This idea is best **specified** by the following example: … | verdeutlichen |

Basisvokabular

first, ... firstly, ... first off, ...	Erstens ...
second, ...	Zweitens ...
third, ...	Drittens ...
furthermore	außerdem, darüber hinaus
moreover	außerdem, darüber hinaus
in addition	außerdem, darüber hinaus
besides	außerdem, darüber hinaus
finally	Schließlich ..., Letztlich ...

Aufbauvokabular und Satzbeispiele

first, ...	**First**, we would like to point out that ...	Erstens ...
firstly, ...	**Firstly**, we would like to point out that ...	
first off, ...	**First off**, we would like to point out that ...	
to begin with	**To begin with**, we would like to give a brief historical survey.	zunächst
then	**Then** it has to be mentioned that ...	dann
furthermore	**Furthermore**, a general sense of the magnitude of certain complications can be obtained from the treatment reported.	außerdem, darüber hinaus
moreover	**Moreover**, a general sense ...	außerdem, darüber hinaus

I. D 3. Aufzählungen

in addition	**In addition**, a general sense … **In addition** to the above, …	außerdem, darüber hinaus
also	**Also**, the energy distributions measured by … were … The following statement is **also** true: …	auch, außerdem **INFO: Also** *kann kei-nen verneinten Satz einleiten.*
other	**Other** issues worth considering are …	andere(s), weitere(s)
another	**Another** important consideration is that most surgeons excluded high-risk individuals. The rise of virus-related deaths is **another** disturbing fact.	andere(s), weitere(s)
besides	**Besides**, there are other advantages that deserve mentioning. There are other previously unknown enzymes **besides** those mentioned above.	außerdem, darüber hinaus neben
finally	**Finally**, we may not forget … **Finally**, it should be noted that …	Schließlich …, Letztlich …
the former **the latter**	Group A showed a significantly lower rate of pulmonary embolism than group B. While **the former** received a high-dose treatment, **the latter** has only been treated according to the traditional low-dose protocol.	erstere(s) letztere(s)

D 4. Beispiele / How to give examples

Basisvokabular

example	Beispiel
for example	zum Beispiel
for instance	zum Beispiel
e.g.	zum Beispiel
like	wie etwa, wie z. B.
such as	wie etwa, wie z. B.
i.e.	d. h.

Aufbauvokabular und Satzbeispiele

example	This is an excellent **example** of the potential power of this technology.	Beispiel
for example	Pike, **for example**, are freshwater predators.	zum Beispiel
	In one case, **for example**, a multi-trauma patient was taken directly to the operating room due to the severe nature of his injuries.	
for instance	Bile duct injury, **for instance**, increased by more than 10% from 1991 to 1998.	zum Beispiel
e.g.	In the course of our analysis we have detected a variety of pitfalls, **e.g.** lack of patient compliance.	zum Beispiel **INFO:** *Die anzuführende Beispielkomponente steht immer <u>nach</u>* **e.g.**
like	Advantages **like** higher resolution and shorter scanning times are obvious.	wie etwa, wie z. B.

I. D 4. Beispiele

such as	Other procedures, **such as** sonography and intravenous cholangiography, have been widely accepted.	wie etwa, wie z. B.
		INFO: Such as zieht i. d. R. mehrere Beispielkomponenten nach sich und wird vornehmlich im BE verwendet. **Like** hingegen ist hier universell verwendbar.
i.e. (*auch* **ie**)	… brings us to an astonishing conclusion, **i.e.** a minor correction to Newton's First Law of Motion.	d. h.

Basisvokabular

to emphasize	betonen
to stress	betonen
to point out	hinweisen (auf)
to foreground	hervorheben
to highlight	hervorheben
to underline	unterstreichen
to focus (on)	sich konzentrieren (auf), den Schwerpunkt setzen bei, den Akzent setzen (auf)
to note	beachten, zur Kenntnis nehmen
above all	vor allem
particular	besonders
considerable	beträchtlich
remarkable	bemerkenswert
important	wichtig

Aufbauvokabular und Satzbeispiele

to emphasize	It is **important** to **emphasize** that …	betonen
to stress	The authors would like to **stress** the importance of …	betonen
to point out	We have to **point out** that any study of this kind is subject to various limitations.	hinweisen (auf)
to foreground	Of 20 related cases we have chosen to **foreground** the following two.	hervorheben

I. D 5. Betonungen und Hervorhebungen

to highlight	In this context it is indispensable to **highlight** the achievements of ancient Chinese medicine. These figures seem very high, and it is tempting to think that only the most extreme cases have been **highlighted**.	hervorheben
to underline	Smith et al. have **underlined** the **essential** role of …	unterstreichen
to underscore	The tragic situation in Mexico **underscored** the inefficiency of …	unterstreichen, betonen
to focus (on)	We **focus on** the pyruvate dehydrogenase complex as described by Patterson.	sich konzentrieren (auf), den Schwerpunkt setzen bei, den Akzent setzen (auf)
to note	It should be **noted**, however, that extra dietary protein will be needed by people suffering from cancer.	beachten, zur Kenntnis nehmen
above all	**Above all**, we must not forget … **Above all**, the aim of such a forum should be to provide the best possible service to children and their families.	vor allem
particular	Of **particular** concern is the role of …	besonders
in particular	**In particular**, it was a widespread opinion that …	insbesondere
particularly	Ebola is a **particularly** nasty form of … The results of our study support this theory, **particularly** when we take a closer look at …	besonders
considerable	There is **considerable** research interest in new treatments.	beträchtlich
remarkable	We note that there is **remarkable** intersubject variability in …	bemerkenswert

to be worth mentioning	In this context steroids are also **worth mentioning**.	bemerkenswert sein
important	Most **important**, in our study, no new sites of metastases were seen on scanning after therapy.	wichtig
special	These findings suggest that the deposition of coating material deserves **special** attention.	besonders, besondere(-n/-s)
impressive	The most **impressive** thing about this report is the fact that …	beeindruckend
significant	The most **significant** outcome gleaned from the data in this study is the …	bedeutend; signifikant
striking	Two **striking** things can be revealed about …	bemerkenswert, hervorstechend, auffällig
essential	For many decades, penicillin has been the **essential** anti-infective drug.	essenziell, wesentlich
critical	Rising ozone levels have played a **critical** role in …	entscheidend, tragend
crucial	The patient has entered a **crucial** stage of his illness.	entscheidend, gravierend (*stärker als* **critical**)
vital	Our data reveal the **vital** role of … in this novel concept.	lebenswichtig, alles entscheidend
paramount	Immediate imaging of the affected vessels is of **paramount** importance. This has turned out to be **paramount** in treating malignant melanoma patients.	alles entscheidend, herausragend

D 6. Vergleiche und Gegenüberstellungen / How to compare and contrast

Basisvokabular

to compare (with)	vergleichen (mit)
to distinguish (between)	unterscheiden (zwischen)
to differentiate (between)	differenzieren (zwischen)
to contrast	gegenüberstellen
on the contrary	im Gegenteil
opposed to	im Gegensatz zu
on the one hand on the other hand	einerseits andererseits
however	jedoch, hingegen
yet	dennoch

Aufbauvokabular und Satzbeispiele

to compare (with)	The side-effects of AIDS wasting may be **compared with** …	vergleichen (mit)
	The results of our study **compare** favourably *(BE)*/favorably *(AE)* **with** those reported in the literature.	
	The major drawback of the laparoscopic procedure relates to its apparent higher bile duct injury rate **compared with** the open procedure.	
	The incidence of hepatic injury in the first 100 patients was 2.0%, (as) **compared with** 1.0% for subsequent patients.	

56

in comparison	**In comparison**, the readmission rates in two series of conventional cholecystectomies were 3 and 5 percent.	im Vergleich (dazu)
comparable	These findings are **comparable** to the 0.5% incidence of bile duct injury observed in the prospective multi-centre *(BE)*/multicenter *(AE)* study of the Southern Surgeons Club.	vergleichbar **INFO:** *Streng genommen bedeutet* **comparable**, *dass sich Dinge zwar vergleichen lassen, aber nicht notwendigerweise ähnlich sein müssen. Im Sprachgebrauch wird* **comparable** *aber häufig synonym zu* **similar** *verwendet (s. Beispielsatz).* **Similar** *ist in diesem Falle bevorzugt zu verwenden.*
similar	These findings are **similar** to those of Smith et al. In a **similar** fashion, the data set from the chest and abdomen may be used to reformat a CT angiogram of the aorta.	ähnlich
identical	Complication rates were **identical** for both groups.	identisch, gleich
to be equal to	The explosion **was equal to** nearly five tons of TNT.	entsprechen
to be the equivalent of	Similarly, the last value of 83 **is the equivalent of** the maximum score.	entsprechen, gleichbedeutend sein
to be congruent with	We have identified aspects and traits, which **are congruent with** a resilient personality.	sich decken mit, übereinstimmen mit
to tally with	These figures **tally with** data from the survey.	übereinstimmen mit

I. D 6. Vergleiche und Gegenüberstellungen

to be on a par with	Teaching Biochemistry must **be** put **on a par with** lab skills in order to teach science effectively.	von gleichrangiger Bedeutung sein auf Augenhöhe mit … sein
to differentiate (between)	Previous studies did not **differentiate between** high-dose and low-dose therapy.	differenzieren (zwischen)
to distinguish (between)	We have to **distinguish between** patient-related and external factors.	unterscheiden (zwischen)
to make a distinction (between)	We have to **make an** important **distinction between** the African and the Asian virus type.	eine Unterscheidung treffen (zwischen)
unlike	**Unlike** previous publications, our research aimed at …	anders als
to contrast	Our aim was to **contrast** non-invasive and surgical therapies.	gegenüberstellen
on the contrary	**On the contrary**, it seems beneficial to group A.	im Gegenteil
contrary to	**Contrary to** the widely held belief that …	entgegen, im Gegensatz zu
in contrast to	This experience stands **in contrast to** concerns raised in the media.	im Widerspruch zu
contradictory	Others have reported **contradictory** findings.	widersprechend, gegenteilig
opposed to	In this analysis, the definition of "academic" as **opposed to** "private practice" surgeons was based on …	im Gegensatz zu
on the one hand **on the other hand**	**On the one hand**, the new procedure has rapidly spread in western countries. **On the other hand**, it has turned out to be irresponsibly expensive.	einerseits andererseits

whereas	It has been stated that paramedics in the United States tend tc conduct onsite emergency surgery, **whereas** their European counterparts prefer traditional hospital care.	wogegen
however	Its clinical value, **however**, has been the subject of intense debate. **However**, there was a high proportion of minor injuries.	jedoch, hingegen
yet	**Yet**, there are certain alarming aspects to consider. **Yet** unlike influenza, for example, SARS shows …	dennoch
nonetheless	**Nonetheless**, CT is still not available around the clock in many facilities.	dennoch, trotzdem
nevertheless	Despite its decreasing popularity, this method is **nevertheless** very effective.	dennoch, trotzdem
still	**Still**, there are unanswered questions and unknown data in respect of substrate binding and enzyme action.	dennoch, trotzdem
despite	**Despite** previously reported advances in nanotechnology, there are still …	trotz
in spite of	**In spite of** previously …	trotz

INFO: Entwicklungen und Veränderungen quantitativer Größen werden im Kapitel D14 ausführlich behandelt.

Basisvokabular

development	Entwicklung
tendency	Tendenz
to increase	zunehmen
to decrease	abnehmen
to improve	(sich) verbessern
to deteriorate	(sich) verschlechtern

Aufbauvokabular und Satzbeispiele

development	This article illustrates the latest **developments** in evolutionary biology.	Entwicklung
tendency	These data show a clear **tendency** towards the use of …	Tendenz
to increase	Drivers who rely on airbag protection alone **increase** their fatality risk exponentially.	zunehmen
to decrease	Complication rates have **decreased** since 1994.	abnehmen
to increase by	This **increased/decreased** the risk of major complications **by** 10%.	erhöhen um, steigern um
to decrease by		erniedrigen um, mindern um

to improve	Far from being optimistic, we have to admit that the overall situation has slightly **improved**.	(sich) verbessern
	However, routine intraoperative cholangiography may **improve** the intraoperative recognition of bile duct injury.	
to enhance	Sanitary systems in these countries will have to be **enhanced** significantly before …	verbessern; *auch*: fördern, steigern, verstärken
to continue	This trend **continues** unabated.	fortführen, weiterlaufen
to deteriorate	The situation in Vietnam is **deteriorating**.	(sich) verschlechtern
to aggravate	These post-operative problems are **aggravated** by the abysmal standard of hygiene and sanitation in Ghana.	verschlechtern
to exacerbate	Rheumatic gonarthritis can be **exacerbated** by bacterial superinfection.	verschlechtern, verschärfen

61

Basisvokabular

to evaluate	einschätzen, beurteilen, bewerten
to assess	einschätzen, beurteilen, bewerten
to estimate	schätzen, abschätzen *(nur bei messbaren/ quantifizierbaren Größen)*
to underestimate	unterschätzen
to overestimate	überschätzen

Aufbauvokabular und Satzbeispiele

to evaluate	The aim of our study was to **evaluate** the effects of hyperthermia on tumour *(BE)*/tumor *(AE)* growth.	einschätzen, beurteilen, bewerten
to assess	In our research, we **assessed** …	einschätzen, beurteilen, bewerten
		INFO: To evaluate *und* to assess *werden hier synonym gebraucht. Bei der Auswertung von Ergebnissen wird nur* to evaluate results *verwendet.*
to assess s.th. for s.th.	Novel alpha-fetoprotein agonists were **assessed** in immortalized cell lines **for** their ability to enhance radioresistant DNA synthesis.	etw. auf etw. hin beurteilen
assessment	With any new procedure, there must be critical **assessment** of the related complications.	Bewertung

to estimate	Without reliable data, the true complication rates can only be **estimated**. **Estimated** figures range from … to …	schätzen, abschätzen
to under- /overestimate	Without reliable data, it is quite easy to run the risk of **under-/overestimating** the effects of this new chemical compound on …	unter-/überschätzen
estimate	Due to a lack of reliable data, the figures obtained are a rough **estimate** at best.	Schätzung **INFO:** Estimate *sollte immer dann verwendet werden, wenn es um numerische Schätzungen geht.* **Estimation** *wird häufig synonym gebraucht, bezeichnet streng genommen aber jegliche Art der Einschätzung (z. B. auch einer Situation).*
to regard s.th. as s.th.	Only five years ago the method was **regarded as** the gold-standard in pain treatment.	etw. für etw. halten/ erachten
to consider s.th. (to be) s.th.	Obesity was initially **considered** (**to be**) a contraindication to the new procedure. This was **considered** (**to be**) unnecessary because of the obvious advantages of the new method.	etw. für etw. halten/ erachten
to believe s.th. to be s.th.	The intramural air in small bowel ischemia is **believed to be** a result of mucosal injury.	etw. für etw. halten/ erachten
to deem s.th. (as) s.th.	Due to these deficiencies in previous studies, we **deem** their findings (**as**) not representative.	etw. für etw. halten/ erachten *(sehr förmlich)*

D 9.1. Ergebnisse anderer Studien / Results of other studies

INFO: *Die Erwähnung anderer Studienergebnisse ist eine sehr häufige Schreib-situation, so dass wir hier ganz bewusst eine große Vielzahl alternativer Formu-lierungsmöglichkeiten anführen. Die Gliederung der Beispielsätze erfolgt deshalb in Abweichung von den übrigen Kapiteln an dieser Stelle auch nicht nach den ver-wendeten Vokabeln, sondern entsprechend ihrer jeweiligen Satzkonstruktion, um eine übersichtlichere und leichter verwendbare Darbietung der Textbausteine zu gewährleisten. Das Vokabular findet sich daher ausschließlich in einem Block am Kapitelanfang.*

Vokabular

to find	feststellen, finden
to show	zeigen
to report	berichten, dokumentieren
to address s.th.	etw. ansprechen
to investigate	untersuchen
to examine	untersuchen
to study	untersuchen
to evaluate	bewerten
to note	verzeichnen
to cite	verzeichnen
to describe	beschreiben
to demonstrate	demonstrieren, zeigen
to indicate	anzeigen, hinweisen (auf)
to suggest	*hier*: vorbringen
to claim	behaupten

to compare	vergleichen
comparison study	Vergleichsstudie, Vergleichsarbeit
to conclude	schlussfolgern

Aufbauvokabular und Satzbeispiele

Satzbeginn mit dem Autor

Smith et al. have **investigated** the influence of …

Smith et al. **found** that …

Smith et al. have **shown** that …

Smith et al. have **demonstrated** that …

Smith et al. have **compared** …

Smith et al. have **studied** …

Smith and coworkers **studied** the value of …

Smith and coworkers **investigated** the use of …

Smith et al. **addressed** several issues in a retrospective analysis of 51 patients with colorectal cancer.

Smith and coworkers **reported** that … They also found that …

Smith and coworkers have **compared** … They found that …

Smith and coworkers **compared** … They found that … The authors concluded that …

Authors of several studies have **shown** that …

Several authors have **shown** that …

Some authors have **demonstrated** that …

Numerous investigators have **demonstrated** …

The authors **concluded** that …

Several authors have **claimed** that …

Others have **suggested** that …

The method has been **described** by several authors with varying reported success.

I. D 9.1. Ergebnisse anderer Studien

Satzbeginn mit der Studie

A study by Smith et al. **showed** …

A study by Smith et al. **suggests** …

A prospective study by Smith et al. **concluded** that …

Studies by Smith and coworkers **suggest** …

In the study by Smith et al. …

In a prospective study from Spain, researchers combined …

In one study, MRI has been **shown** to be a sensitive method for evaluating …

In all these studies, PET was superior to CT for detection of lymph node metastases.

The studies that have been published deal primarily with …

Other series have **noted** postoperative bile leak rates of 0.2% to 2.0%.

Single and multi-institutional experiences have **cited** rates of 0% to 2%.

The data that do exist **indicate** that …

Some studies have **indicated** an overestimation of the standardized uptake value in the presence of CT contrast material.

Previous studies **describe** an overall morbidity rate of …

Previous studies have **indicated** that …

Previous experience has **demonstrated** that …

A previous report by Moore and colleagues in a cohort of 24 patients **demonstrated** good agreement between the two methods.

Viele und wenige Vergleichsstudien

A large body of literature exists that **demonstrates** the use of …

There is extensive literature concerning the role of …

There are numerous case reports in which …

In most studies, PET is more accurate for … than …

The results of most studies **indicate** that …

The vast majority of clinical studies …

Most studies **suggest** that higher FDG uptake is correlated with more clinically aggressive behaviour.

Several studies have **demonstrated** …

Several studies have **shown** …

Several studies have **evaluated** the use of …

Several **comparison studies** have proven that …

Several large published series have **reported** their initial experience with …

Several reviews have covered general and epilepsy-related aspects of PET methodology in detail.

Relatively few studies have been performed to directly compare …

Few studies have **examined** the role of PET in the detection of …

Only a few studies have **evaluated** the role of …

There are few articles in the literature in which …

Three studies have been performed to **evaluate** …

To date, no study of which we are aware has **evaluated** the use of FDG PET in the diagnosis of …

… because there are currently only very limited published data on the use of PET/CT for treatment monitoring with new tracers.

As the number of such studies is still very limited, it is currently not possible to draw firm conclusions about whether PET/CT makes a difference.

In patients without clinical evidence of metastases, there is only minimal literature supporting the routine use of FDG-PET.

To date, no large multicentre *(BE)*/multicenter *(AE)* trials have been published to confirm the value of …

Although only a limited number of studies have **evaluated** the role of …, certain indications are evident.

To our knowledge, no studies have **compared** …

I. D 9.1. Ergebnisse anderer Studien

Ältere und neuere Vergleichsstudien

Initial findings **suggested** that …

Initial studies using FET PET for the analysis of brain tumours *(BE)*/tumors *(AE)* have **shown** results similar to those obtained with MET PET.

The results of early studies supported a strong role for PET in evaluation of …

In an early study, …

In three recent studies, the sensitivity of … ranged between 62% and 78%.

In a recent survey in the United States, …

In a recent article, 60 patients with ovarian carcinoma were **evaluated** for …

More recently, these investigators **showed** that …

A more recent study **showed** …

Recent studies have **shown** that …

Data from several recent reports **indicate** that …

A recent study by Smith et al. **showed** …

Andere Varianten

Interest has recently been focused on …

On the basis of prior publications, we might expect …

A systematic review of the PET literature by Smith and coworkers **concluded** that …

An analysis of published data reveals …

The published literature **suggests** that …

It remains a highly morbid disorder with **reported** mortality rates of 40%.

Basisvokabular

to correlate with	korrelieren mit
to correspond with	entsprechen
to be consistent with	übereinstimmen mit
in accordance with	in Übereinstimmung mit
in agreement with	in Übereinstimmung mit
concordant with	übereinstimmend/konkordant mit
in line with	in Übereinstimmung mit
in keeping with	in Übereinstimmung mit

Aufbauvokabular und Satzbeispiele

to correlate with	These results **correlate** well **with** the literature.	korrelieren mit
to correspond with	A major morbidity rate of 2% **corresponds with** the overall complication rates of 2% to 11% that have been reported.	entsprechen
to be consistent with	Our results **are consistent with** those reported by Smith et al. Our results **are consistent with** a recent study …	übereinstimmen mit
in accordance with	This observation is **in accordance with** Smith et al. (2), who reported …	in Übereinstimmung mit
in agreement with	**In agreement with** the findings in previous studies, we found that … These results are **in** close **agreement with** those obtained by Moore et al.	in Übereinstimmung mit

I. D 9.2. Gemeinsamkeiten

concordant with	Our data is **concordant with** those of previous studies.	übereinstimmend/kon-kordant mit
in line with	Our results are **in line with** data from the literature.	in Übereinstimmung mit
in keeping with	These results are **in keeping with** previous studies, which reported that …	in Übereinstimmung mit
s.th. compares favourably *(BE)/* **favorably** *(AE)* **with s.th.**	These results **compare favourably** *(BE)/***favorably** *(AE)* **with** those reported in the literature.	etw. ist gut mit etw. vergleichbar (*i. S. v.* nicht abweichen von)
comparable	This review of available data on rainfall and drought frequency reveals **comparable** results.	vergleichbar **INFO:** *Streng genommen bedeutet* **comparable**, *dass sich Dinge zwar vergleichen lassen, aber nicht notwendigerweise ähnlich sein müssen. Im Sprachgebrauch wird* **comparable** *aber häufig synonym zu* **similar** *verwendet (s. Beispielsatz).* **Similar** *ist in diesem Falle eigentlich bevorzugt zu verwenden.*
similar	**Similar** findings were reported by … **Similar** results have been demonstrated by Smith and coworkers. Many studies have reported **similar** results.	ähnlich
to confirm	These data were **confirmed** by Smith and coworkers.	bestätigen

D 9.3. Unterschiede / Differences

INFO: *Vgl. hierzu Kapitel D6.*

Basisvokabular

different	anders, unterschiedlich
to take a different view (on)	eine unterschiedliche Haltung einnehmen
to differ from	sich unterscheiden von
to deviate (from)	abweichen (von)
to vary (from)	abweichen (von)
to contradict	widersprechen
contradictory	widersprechend, gegenteilig
in contrast to	im Gegensatz zu
to disagree (with)	nicht zustimmen, anderer Meinung sein

Aufbauvokabular und Satzbeispiele

different	Earlier studies have reported **different** results. Several recent studies with the same or closely related methods have come to very **different** conclusions.	anders, unterschiedlich
to take a different view (on)	Smith et al. **take a different view on** the importance of …	eine unterschiedliche Haltung einnehmen
to differ from	Our findings **differ from** previously recorded data. The number of severe injuries did not **differ from** that reported by others.	sich unterscheiden von

71

I. D 9.3. Unterschiede

to deviate (from)	Initial figures **deviate** to a large extent **from** data gathered during a recent simulation despite unaltered parameters.	abweichen (von)
to vary (from)	The results of recent multicentre *(BE)*/ multicenter *(AE)* studies strongly **vary from** those obtained in 1998.	abweichen (von)
to contradict	One feels tempted to categorically **contradict** all findings in the 1992 study.	widersprechen
contradictory	Comparison studies have reported **contradictory** findings.	widersprechend, gegenteilig
in contrast to	**In contrast to** U.S. standards we have chosen to abide by the standard values set by European researchers. **In contrast to** these earlier findings we observed … This finding is **in contrast to** other published data demonstrating an advantage of PET over CT.	im Gegensatz zu
to disagree (with)	As far as our Asian control group's findings are concerned we strongly **disagree with** the way these results have been obtained.	nicht zustimmen, anderer Meinung sein

D 10. Beweisführung / How to argue

D 10.1. Ursachenanalyse / Causal analysis

Basisvokabular

because of	wegen, aufgrund von
caused by	verursacht von, begründet durch
to result from	resultieren aus
to originate from	herrühren von
to stem from	herrühren von
due to	wegen, aufgrund von
owing to	wegen, aufgrund von
to relate to	bedingt sein durch, abhängen von, *auch*: zusammenhängen mit
to attribute to	zurückführen auf
attributable to	zurückzuführen auf
as a consequence	folglich

Aufbauvokabular und Satzbeispiele

because of	It is **because of** negligence in sanitary matters that diseases like cholera are on the rise.	wegen, aufgrund von
caused by	The increase in lethal cases of cholera is **caused by** …	verursacht von, begründet durch
to result from	Such strictures may **result from** inflammation and fibrosis due to bile leak. 18 out of 33 postoperative deaths **resulted from** operative injury.	resultieren aus

73

I. D 10.1. Ursachenanalyse

to originate from	The higher number of wound infections **originates from** the preselection of patients in group B.	herrühren von
to stem from	This widespread view **stems from** a fatal misinterpretation of basic conditions.	herrühren von
due to	This may be **due to** increased levels of …	wegen, aufgrund von
owing to	**Owing to** the ongoing depletion of natural resources, alternative ways of generating electricity will play a crucial role.	wegen, aufgrund von
to relate to	The major drawback of this technique **relates to** its apparently higher costs. These changes **relate to** a number of factors, including patient convenience and lower costs. A significant proportion of operative deaths are **related to** technical complications.	bedingt sein durch, abhängen von, *auch*: zusammenhängen mit
to attribute to	No complications were **attributed** directly **to** laser-surgical techniques. The differences in remission rates between our study and the previous survey can be **attributed to** differences in study design. This fact might also be **attributed**, in part, **to** …	zurückführen auf
attributable to	Nonetheless, more than half of the reported deaths were **attributable to** a technical complication.	zurückzuführen auf
as a consequence	**As a consequence**, we chose a different approach.	folglich
apparent	The advantages of method A are **apparent**.	offensichtlich

obvious	It is **obvious** that the same vaccines frequently show different results in different patients.	offensichtlich
evident	The advantages of the new concept are **evident**: …	offensichtlich, auf der Hand liegend
clear	It is **clear** that … The reasons for this increase are not made **clear** by the present study.	eindeutig, klar
multifactorial	The high mortality is **multifactorial**, but it is often related to a delay in diagnosis.	multifaktoriell
to combine (to)	These factors **combine to** significantly improve image quality.	zusammenwirken
to contribute to	The late recognition of these injuries in patients with sepsis and peritonitis **contributes to** the relatively high associated mortality.	beitragen zu, bedingen
to explain	Biased selection **explains** the differences between …	erklären
to be explained (by)	The increase **is explained by** …	sich erklären (durch)
explanation	Possible **explanations** for the differences are …	Erklärung
responsible (for)	Bacteria are partially **responsible for** the anaerobic decomposition of sludge.	verantwortlich (für)
therefore	It is **therefore** imperative for us to use … **Therefore**, it is imperative …	deswegen, deshalb
hence	…; **hence**, it is imperative, that we use …	deswegen, deshalb
for this reason	**For this reason**, we decided to form three subgroups.	aus diesem Grund

I. D 10.1. Ursachenanalyse

that is (the reason) why ...	**That is the reason why** this vicious form of Ebola is still on the rise.	deswegen, aus diesem Grund, darum
on account of	**On account of** recent data obtained by Dr Smith we have been able to enhance the detection of gamma rays.	aufgrund von, wegen

Basisvokabular

to show	zeigen
to indicate	hinweisen (auf)
to demonstrate	zeigen, demonstrieren
to prove	beweisen, bestätigen
to support	unterstützen
to confirm	bestätigen, bekräftigen
to corroborate	bekräftigen, untermauern (*stärker als* **to confirm**)
to provide an argument for s.th.	ein Argument für etw. liefern
to provide support for s.th.	Unterstützung bieten
to advocate	befürworten
to endorse	befürworten, gutheißen, *auch*: absegnen (*i. S. v.* genehmigen)

Aufbauvokabular und Satzbeispiele

to show	This study clearly **shows** that there is no difference in the safety of this procedure whether it is performed in an academic or a private hospital. In summary, our results clearly **show** that …	zeigen
to indicate	Our experience **indicated** that the thinner-section reconstructions are redundant. These results **indicate** that …	hinweisen (auf)

I. D 10.2. Pro

to demonstrate	This study **demonstrates** a marked increase in the frequency of …	zeigen, demonstrieren
	These data **demonstrate** that laparoscopic appendectomy is essentially a safe procedure.	
to prove	These findings **prove** our hypothesis of …	beweisen, bestätigen
	Our research has **proven** that …	
ample evidence	We believe to have gathered **ample evidence** to verify our theory.	ausreichende Beweise
to support	The existence of a learning curve for the novel method is clearly **supported** by this study.	unterstützen
	The findings of this study **support** the assumption that …	
to confirm	This review **confirms** previously held notions, such as …	bestätigen, bekräftigen
	This study has **confirmed** the presence of a wide range of …	
	Our data **confirm** and expand previous observations.	
to corroborate	Our data **corroborate** the trend towards minimally-invasive techniques in gallstone surgery.	bekräftigen, untermauern (*stärker als* **to confirm**)
to provide an argument for s.th.	These results **provide a** strong **argument for** …	ein Argument für etw. liefern
to provide support for s.th.	These studies **provide support for** the hypothesis that …	Unterstützung bieten
to advocate	This approach can be most strongly **advocated** when symptoms are poorly localized.	befürworten
to endorse	These guidelines have been **endorsed** by the following institutions: …	befürworten, gutheißen, *auch*: absegnen (*i. S. v.* genehmigen)

to be in favour *(BE)*/**favor** *(AE)* **of s.th.**	Our team **is in favour** *(BE)*/**favor of** *(AE)* a more restricted use of the novel method.	für etw. sein
to favour *(BE)*/ **favor** *(AE)* **s.th.**	We clearly **favour** *(BE)*/**favor** *(AE)* the Scandinavian solution.	befürworten, favorisieren
to approve of s.th.	The Society for … has **approved of** the recommendation to …	befürworten, begrüßen **INFO:** *Im Zusammenhang mit einem Genehmigungsverfahren sollte* **to approve s.th.** *verwendet werden* (The Ethics Committee has **approved** the study protocol).
to give one's approval to	Federal antitrust authorities **have given their approval to** DocPerry's purchase of the ailing Texan Biotech-4-All company.	billigen, zustimmen
to lend countenance to	We therefore **lend countenance to** a more widespread use of …	billigen, unterstützen

D 10.3. Contra / How to argue against s.th.

Basisvokabular

to criticize	kritisieren
to disagree (with)	nicht einverstanden sein (mit)
to be against s.th.	gegen etw. sein
to disapprove of s.th.	etw. missbilligen, nicht befürworten
to object to s.th.	etw. ablehnen, widersprechen
to reject s.th.	etw. ablehnen, zurückweisen
to disprove s.th.	etw. widerlegen

Aufbauvokabular und Satzbeispiele

to criticize	This model has been **criticized** in many recent publications.	kritisieren
to disagree (with)	Based upon the results of this study we **disagree with** previously published recommendations …	nicht einverstander sein (mit)
to be against s.th.	For the above-mentioned reasons we **are against** a renaissance of metformin.	gegen etw. sein
to disapprove of s.th.	We therefore **disapprove of** the conventional technique that is still practised (BE)/practiced (AE) in many smaller community hospitals.	etw. missbilligen, nicht befürworten
to object to s.th.	As our results demonstrate an obvious advantage of the laser technique, we **object to** a continued use of the conventional device.	etw. ablehnen, widersprechen
to reject s.th.	On the basis of our data, we have to **reject** Meyer's theory.	etw. ablehnen, zurückweisen

to disprove s.th.	The conclusions drawn from previous studies are **disproven** by our results.	etw. widerlegen
to harbour *(BE)/* **harbor** *(AE)* **doubts about s.th.**	We **harbour** *(BE)/***harbor** *(AE)* some **doubts about** the validity of these data.	Zweifel an etw. hegen
to raise doubts about s.th.	These data **raise doubts about** …	Zweifel an etw. aufwerfen
to raise concern about s.th.	These data **raise concern about** …	Bedenken bezüglich etw. aufwerfen
to raise ques- tions about s.th.	These data **raise questions about** …	Fragen über etw. auf- werfen
to question s.th.	As a result of our findings, we **question** the widespread model of …	etw. in Frage stellen
to challenge s.th.	The classic model was first **chal- lenged** when …	etw. in Frage stellen (*stärker als* **to question s.th.**)
	The present data do **not support** this assumption. This trend in the results did **not support** our hypothesis. Our data do **not confirm** the efficacy of …	**INFO:** *Die nebenste- henden Beispielsätze beinhalten kein neues Vokabular. Sie stellen lediglich weitere the- menbezogene Formu- lierungsmöglichkeiten dar. Vollständige Ver- neinung der positiv belegten Verben aus dem Kapitel* **D 10.2 Pro / How to argue for s.th.** *als Mittel der Gegenargumentation.*

Basisvokabular

to conclude	schlussfolgern, *auch*: abschließend
conclusion	Schlussfolgerung
in conclusion	somit, folglich, *auch*: abschließend
as a consequence	folglich
thus	folglich, deswegen
hence	deswegen
therefore	deswegen

Aufbauvokabular und Satzbeispiele

to conclude	We **conclude** that this technology offers a number of benefits to …	schlussfolgern
	On the basis of the data from this study, we **conclude** that …	abschließend
	To conclude, we would like to mention …	
conclusion	The results of these studies are consistent with the following **conclusions**.	Schlussfolgerung
in conclusion	**In conclusion**, a significant decrease of complications could be achieved by using the new technique.	somit, folglich, *auch*: abschließend
finally	**Finally**, pulsed power technology for the active detection of special nuclear materials is either exorbitantly expensive or widely unavailable.	abschließend, schließlich, und zuletzt

consequently	**Consequently**, the positions of the lungs and liver are likely to differ between PET and CT images.	folglich
as a consequence	**As a consequence** of our findings, we recommend that …	folglich
thus	**Thus**, the new procedure accounts for less complications than … Theory A has **thus** been proven correct.	folglich, deswegen
hence	…; **hence**, this assessment cannot be neglected.	deswegen
therefore	We **therefore** advocate systematic surgical training.	deswegen
to indicate	We believe that this study **indicates** that … A comparison of the results obtained after the first cycle and the completion of chemotherapy **indicated** a statistically significant difference in … These results **indicate** that … This study **indicates** that …	zeigen, hinweisen (auf)
as a result	**As a result**, mortality was cut in half.	im Ergebnis

D 11. Zusammenhänge / How to explain relations

Basisvokabular

to be associated with	etw. mit sich bringen, mit etw. zusammenhängen
to be related to	mit etw. zusammenhängen, *auch*: durch etw. verursacht werden
to be based on	basieren auf
to depend on	abhängen von
as for s.th.	was etw. angeht
with respect to	im Hinblick auf, unter Berücksichtigung von
with regard to	im Hinblick auf
context	Zusammenhang
to influence	beeinflussen
to affect	beeinflussen

Aufbauvokabular und Satzbeispiele

to be associated with	Increasing age **is associated with** increasing risks of postoperative complications.	etw. mit sich bringen, mit etw. zusammenhängen
to be related to	The degree to which the image is degraded **is related to** a number of parameters. They provided detailed information on all complications **related to** the new treatment.	mit etw. zusammenhängen, *auch*: durch etw. verursacht werden
to be based on	The conclusions drawn in recent studies **are** not always **based on** facts.	basieren auf

84

to depend on	In this clinical setting, survival rates strongly **depend on** the time until coronary angioplasty is successfully completed.	abhängen von
as for s.th.	**As for** the frequency count for each interval, it is located at the top of each box. **As for** photosynthesis, we found …	was etw. angeht
independent of	**Independent of** the increasing number of AIDS-related deaths, governmental measures to prevent further infections are still delayed.	unabhängig von
together with	These fractures often occur **together with** splenic injuries.	zusammen mit
coupled with	These fractures often occur **coupled with** splenic injuries.	zusammen mit
along with	These fractures often occur **along with** splenic injuries.	zusammen mit
in conjunction with	These fractures often occur **in conjunction with** splenic injuries.	zusammen mit, in Verbindung mit
in tandem with	Reconstruction was programmed into the scanner prospectively where possible so that processing occurred **in tandem with** image collection.	gleichzeitig mit, parallel
to be accompanied by	The postoperative course **was accompanied by** serious complications in less than 2% of the operations.	begleitet werden von
in the absence of	**In the absence of** reliable data, any evaluation of this approach is rather difficult.	ohne, aufgrund fehlender, in Abwesenheit von

I. D 11. Zusammenhänge

with respect to	The technique can be further opti-mized **with respect to** its industrial use.	im Hinblick auf, unter Berücksichtigung von
	The results of method A compare favourably *(BE)*/favorably *(AE)* with those of method B **with respect to** mortality, complications, and length of hospital stay.	
	Patient selection **with respect to** age or gender did not affect the compli-cation rate.	
in this respect	**In this respect**, antibody production is disadvantageous.	in dieser Hinsicht
in respect of	Therefore, this method has several advantages **in respect of** cost-ef-fectiveness.	hinsichtlich
concerning	Therefore, this method has several advantages **concerning** cost-effec-tiveness.	hinsichtlich
pertaining to	A detailed review of the various studies **pertaining to** the use of PET in restaging of various cancer types is beyond the scope of this article.	bezüglich
with regard to	Data was summarized **with regard to** overall morbidity, mortality, length of hospital stay, and duration of postoperative recovery.	im Hinblick auf
context	In this **context**, our data demonstrate that intermolecular contacts can be modified by …	Zusammenhang
regardless of	All subjects have shown identical reactions **regardless of** their age.	ungeachtet
in terms of	The advantages of endoscopic sur-gical procedures **in terms of** reduced postoperative pain have been readily apparent.	*i. S. v.* „was etw. angeht"

as far as s.th. is concerned	**As far as** photosynthesis **is concerned**, we found …	was etw. angeht
bearing (on)	These restrictions had some **bearing on** our study design.	(geringe) Auswirkung (auf), *auch*: Bezug zu
to influence	The introduction of multislice CT has strongly **influenced** cardiac imaging procedures.	beeinflussen
to affect	We have yet to determine how .. **affects** marine wildlife.	beeinflussen
effect (on)	The long-term **effects** of waste disposal have not been thoroughly investigated.	Einfluss (auf), Auswirkung (auf)
impact (on)	These technical improvements had an **impact on** surgical strategies in seriously injured patients.	(starker) Einfluss (auf), (erhebliche) Auswirkung (auf)

D 12. Vermutungen / How to assume

Basisvokabular

to assume	annehmen, vermuten
assumption	Vermutung
to presume	annehmen, vermuten
to suppose	annehmen, davon ausgehen, der Ansicht sein
to suggest	vermuten (lassen)
to estimate	schätzen
to underestimate	unterschätzen
to overestimate	überschätzen

Aufbauvokabular und Satzbeispiele

to assume	The short hospital stay can be **assumed** to indicate the early resumption of normal activities.	annehmen, vermuten
assumption	Based on the **assumption** that … The findings of this study support the **assumption** that …	Vermutung
to presume	We **presume** that these findings are closely related to …	annehmen, vermuten
to suppose	We might **suppose** magnetic resonance imaging to be the dominating imaging modality of the new millennium.	annehmen, davon ausgehen, der Ansicht sein
to suggest	The data **suggest** that … It has been **suggested** that … Our results **suggest** that …	vermuten (lassen)

to estimate	We may confidently **estimate** 13.5% of the overall Nigerian population to suffer from …	schätzen
to underestimate to overestimate	The low operative mortality rate of 0.04% may **underestimate** the true mortality.	unterschätzen überschätzen

D 13. Meinungen / How to express opinions

Basisvokabular

opinion	Meinung
view	Ansicht
to maintain	behaupten
to claim	behaupten
to assert	behaupten
to contend	behaupten, verfechten

Aufbauvokabular und Satzbeispiele

In our opinion **In our view**	In our opinion/view, patients do not benefit from …	Unserer Meinung nach Unserer Ansicht nach
to hold the view that …	Other authors **hold the view that** …	der Ansicht sein, dass …
to maintain	Smith et al. **maintain** that the procedure is cost-effective.	behaupten
to claim	We do not **claim** that …	behaupten
to assert	We **assert** method B to be the primary choice for …	behaupten
to contend	They **contend** that rising complications are due to …	behaupten, verfechten
to be convinced (of s.th./that)	We **are convinced of** the superiority of the novel technique. We **are convinced that** the novel technique is going to replace its predecessor.	(von etw.) überzeugt sein überzeugt sein(, dass …)

It is my contention that …	**It is my contention that** every patient presenting with nausea should …	Meiner festen Überzeugung nach …
In our experience …	**In our experience**, magnetic resonance imaging does not provide any additional information in the setting of gastrointestinal bleeding.	Nach unserer Erfahrung …
to believe	We **believe** that …	glauben

D 14. Mengenangaben (weiterführend) / How to use quantities (advanced)

Basisvokabular

major	schwerwiegend, Haupt…, hauptsächlich
minor	gering
more	mehr
less	weniger
increase	Anstieg, Steigerung
decrease	Reduktion, Abfall
frequent	häufig
rare	selten, sporadisch
main	Haupt…, hauptsächlich
mainly	hauptsächlich
largely	überwiegend, größtenteils

Aufbauvokabular und Satzbeispiele

major	Lack of hygiene is a **major** contributing factor to …	schwerwiegend, Haupt…, hauptsächlich
minor	All complications were reported, even such **minor** ones as …	gering
more	**More** than half of the subjects received …	mehr
less	**Less** than half of the samples showed signs of …	weniger
	The postoperative course was accompanied by serious complications in **less** than 2% of the operations.	

increase	The **increase** in complication rates is attributed to …	Anstieg, Steigerung
to increase	We have **increased** the energy efficiency of these batteries by 14%.	steigern, ansteigen
gain	There is a significant **gain** in sensitivity …	Zugewinn, Anstieg
decrease	A significant **decrease** in trace element concentration occurred after …	Reduktion, Abfall
to decrease	Thermal stability has **decreased** due to …	abnehmen
decline	Recently, there has been a significant **decline** in such cases.	Abnahme
to decline	Nutrient supply **declines** rapidly in areas of …	abnehmen, (ab)sinken
frequent	This was a **frequent** complication of the traditional technique.	häufig
frequently	Bile duct injury occurs more **frequently** among patients with acute cholecystitis.	häufig
frequency	The **frequency** of volcanic activity in the designated area is extremely low.	Häufigkeit
rare	One of the **rare** findings was …	selten, sporadisch
rarely	3 groups performed phlebography either **rarely** or not at all.	selten, sporadisch
slight	Bacterial cell density showed only a **slight** difference after …	geringfügig
slightly	A **slightly** higher incidence of …	
marginal	Deviation from the set value was **marginal**.	geringfügig, marginal, *auch*: zu vernachlässigen
marginally	A **marginally** higher rate of …	

I. D 14. Mengenangaben (weiterführend)

main	The **main** advantage lies in continuous data acquisition.	Haupt…, hauptsächlich
mainly	Some methodological deficits, **mainly** the low number of patients, have to be named here.	hauptsächlich
largely	Current reports of laparoscopic cholecystectomy **largely** reflect the experience of early practitioners.	überwiegend, größtenteils
in large part	The high mortality rate associated with this disorder has not changed significantly over the past decades, **in large part** owing to delayed diagnosis.	zu einem großen Teil
for the most part	These published series represent, **for the most part**, the initial experience with laparoscopic cholecystectomy by each reporting institution. **For the most part**, image quality was very good.	zum größten Teil, größtenteils
predominantly	Soil microbiology **predominantly** deals with …	vorwiegend
vast	The **vast** majority of ischemic strokes results from …	groß, überwiegend
considerable	There are **considerable** variations between different institutions.	beträchtlich
extensive	Surgeons who learn the new procedure in the future will no longer have **extensive** experience with traditional techniques.	weitreichend
extent (of)	The **extent** to which guanidine salts act as antiviral agents has yet to be determined. The **extent of** climatic changes related to the continued use of fossil fuels is difficult to measure.	Ausmaß (von), Tragweite

degree	The **degree** to which image quality is enhanced, strongly depends on patient positioning.	Grad
to vary from ... to ...	Contemporary rates of bile duct injury during open cholecystectomy **vary from** 0% **to** 0.4% and are often c ted at 0.1% to 0.25%.	von ... bis ... variieren, von ... bis ... schwanken
to range from ... to ...	The reported death rates **range from** 0% **to** 0.4%.	von ... bis ... reichen
variability	We note that there is considerab e intersubject **variability** in ...	Vielfalt, Variabilität
variation	There is significant **variation** in ...	Variabilität, Schwankungsbreite **INFO:** *Im Zusammenhang mit statistischen Daten verwendet man bevorzugt* **variation**. **Variability** *wird jedoch häufig in diesem Kontext synonym benützt.*
to exceed	The safety of this method remains doubtful, with reintervent on rates **exceeding** 40%. These results have **exceeded** our initial expectations by far.	übersteigen, übertreffen
to minimize	We can, however, **minimize** artefacts by careful positioning of the artefact-causing structures.	minimieren
to maximize	Efficiency can be **maximized** by using ...	maximieren

Basisvokabular

past	vergangen, *auch*: Vergangenheit
previous	vorhergehend, früher
recent	kürzlich
so far	bis jetzt
to date	bislang, bisher
present	gegenwärtig; *bei Daten auch*: vorliegend
current	gegenwärtig, aktuell
future	zukünftig, *auch*: Zukunft
initial(ly)	anfänglich
final	abschließend, endgültig

Aufbauvokabular und Satzbeispiele

past	These issues were intensively discussed in the **past**.	vergangen, *auch*: Vergangenheit
previous	**Previous** studies have reported comparable results.	vorhergehend, früher
recent	In a **recent** study, Smith et al. conclude that …	kürzlich
so far	**So far**, no comparable technique has been implemented. No comparable technique has been implemented **so far**.	bis jetzt

thus far	More than half of the patients should have shown signs of recovery at this stage but they haven't done so, **thus far**.	bis jetzt
		INFO: *Stilistisch höher anzusetzen als* **so far**. *Gebräuchlich zur Vermeidung eines doppelten* **so**.
to date	This the largest series **to date** ... We have not identified, **to date**, any late bile duct complications.	bislang, bisher
present	The **present** data suggest that ..	gegenwärtig; *bei Daten auch*: vorliegend
current	**Current** reports of laparoscopic sigmoidectomy largely reflect the experience of early practitioners.	gegenwärtig, aktuell
future	Whether the use of combined PET/CT-systems is cost-effective will be subject to **future** investigation.	zukünftig, *auch*: Zukunft
initial(ly)	These results reflect the **initial** experience of each surgeon. Obesity was **initially** considered a contraindication to the endoscopic procedure.	anfänglich
final	The **final** version includes several important guidelines.	abschließend, endgültig

Basisvokabular

to go into detail	ins Detail gehen
in detail	detailliert
to detail (s.th.)	etw. genauer erläutern, etw. detailliert erläutern
detailed	detailliert
thorough	gründlich, tiefschürfend
meticulous	(äußerst) sorgfältig, (äußerst) gründlich
extensive	umfassend, weitreichend
exhaustive	erschöpfend, eingehend
intensive	intensiv
to take a closer look at s.th.	etw. genauer betrachten

Aufbauvokabular und Satzbeispiele

to go into detail	We don't have to go into detail to recognize that …	ins Detail gehen
in detail	We have researched the progress of this disease in great detail.	detailliert
to detail (s.th.)	Table 1 details the range of the lateral atlanto-dental interval asymmetry.	etw. genauer erläutern, etw. detailliert erläutern
detailed	Smith et al. have given a detailed description of the underlying bio-chemical interactions.	detailliert
thorough	A thorough analysis of … has yielded the subsequent results.	gründlich, tiefschürfend
meticulous	A meticulous analysis of …	(äußerst) sorgfältig, (äußerst) gründlich

extensive	Here we conduct an **extensive** investigation of …	umfassend, weitreichend
exhaustive	An **exhaustive** description of …	erschöpfend, eingehend
intensive	Despite **intensive** research, the architecture of … remains poorly understood.	intensiv
to take a closer look at s.th.	**Taking a closer look at** acetogenesis, we have to admit that …	etw. genauer betrachten
a closer examination	**A closer examination** of 27 major bile duct injuries in this report revealed that 67% occurred within each individual surgeon's first 25 cases.	eine eingehende Untersuchung
to scrutinize	The complex interaction between … and … was **scrutinized** by Smith et al.	(genauestens) erforschen, (genauestens) untersuchen
to focus on s.th.	In our analysis, we **focused/focussed on** those patients who …	sich mit etw. besonders befassen/auseinandersetzen, sich auf etw. konzentrieren
		INFO: *Beide Schreibweisen sind gebräuchlich.*
a minute detail	But that is nothing more than **a minute detail**.	ein unbedeutendes Detail, ein winziges Detail

INFO: *Da die nachfolgenden Vokabeln für dieses Kapitel von gleichrangiger Bedeutung sind, wird auf eine Unterteilung in Basis- und Aufbauvokabular verzichtet.*

limitation	This study had (certain) **limitations**.	Limitierung
	Several **limitations** should be pointed out in the current study.	
	Small sample size was the major **limitation** of this study.	
	As a **limitation** of the study, only 8 nodules were smaller than 10 millimetres.	
	One **limitation** of the present study is the small number of …	
inherent	These are **inherent limitations** of our study.	innewohnend, natürlich, inhärent
	This study is subject to the **inherent limitations** of any survey-based data.	
to encounter limitations	While these advantages are important, some **limitations were encountered**.	an Grenzen stoßen
to be limited (by)	Our study, like others, **was limited by** the inability to prove with certainty the metastatic nature of all lesions detected with positron emission tomography.	limitiert sein (durch)
problem	One **problem inherent** in a study of this kind is the definition of surgical complications.	Problem
to face a problem	When we set out to investigate the phenomenon of …, we had to **face** three major **problems**.	einem Problem gegenüberstehen

I. D 17. Probleme und Limitierungen der Studie

to be faced with a problem	In adopting the whole-body scan approach, we **were faced with the problem** of the upper extremities.	mit einem Problem konfrontiert werden
shortcoming	One **shortcoming** of our study is the fact that, for ethical reasons, biopsies could only be taken from brain areas that appeared abnormal cn MRI images.	Schwachpunkt, Mangel
drawback	Another **drawback** is the lack of histological confirmation in nine patients.	Manko, Missstand

D 18. Ausblick / Prospects

INFO: In diesem Kapitel werden lediglich einige mögliche Formulierungsalterna-tiven zum Thema dargeboten. Ein spezifisches Vokabular ist hierfür nicht erfor-derlich.

Future studies will be necessary to evaluate the effect of …

Future studies will have to show whether PET can replace conventional imaging in patients with …

It will be an issue/an aim/a goal of future studies to determine the clinical use of …

Further studies are necessary to …

Further studies are needed to …

A larger patient population will have to be examined in order to define the advantages of MRI over CT in these patients.

Prospective studies with large patient groups are essential to further evaluate the cost-effectiveness of this method.

The effect of PET on radiation therapy planning can only be determined by large prospective studies.

Prospective studies should be done to generate data sufficient for the development of guidelines on the use of FDG-PET.

The results of our study indicate that … yet a larger number of patients need to be probed to clearly define the role of …

Well-designed prospective trials may ultimately answer the question about the utility of MRI in these patients.

Whether this method is sufficient to [+ verb]/for [+noun] … remains unde-termined.

The limitations of this study can only

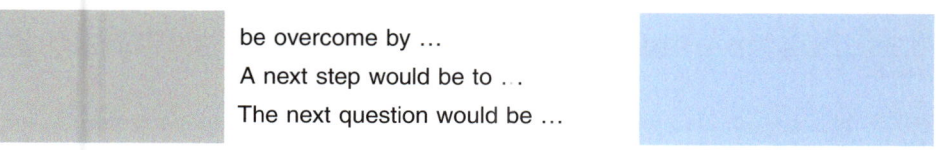

be overcome by …

A next step would be to …

The next question would be …

Zusammenfassung / Summary

INFO: *Thematisch verwandte Vokabeln und Formulierungsbeispiele finder Sie im Kapitel D 10.4. „Schlussfolgerungen / How to draw conclusions".*

Basisvokabular

in summary	zusammengefasst, alles in allem
to sum up	zusammenfassen, zusammenfassend
to summarize	zusammenfassen
finally	abschließend, schließlich
overall	insgesamt
in conclusion	am Ende, schließlich
to conclude	abschließend, *auch*: schlussfolgern

Aufbauvokabular und Satzbeispiele

in summary	**In summary**, our results clearly showed that …	zusammengefasst, alles in allem
to sum up	**To sum up**, digital radiography has successfully replaced conventional imaging systems in our institution.	zusammenfassen, zusammenfassend
summing up	**Summing up**, the results of this large national survey demonstrate that laparoscopic cholecystectomy is essentially a safe procedure with low morbidity and mortality rates.	zusammenfassend
to summarize	Our results can be **summarized** as follows: …	zusammenfassen
finally	**Finally**, the results of this study lead us to the conclusion that …	abschließend, schließlich
overall	**Overall**, this investigation showed that …	insgesamt

in conclusion	**In conclusion**, we may postulate that …	am Ende, schließlich
to conclude	**To conclude**, we strongly recommend interventional procedures for patients who …	abschließend, *auch*: schlussfolgern
in a final analysis	**In a final analysis**, these results demonstrate …	abschließend betrachtet
on the whole	**On the whole**, early surgery in case of suspected small bowel ischem a has lead to …	alles in allem

Basisvokabular

acknowledgement *(BE)/* **acknowledgment** *(AE)*	Anerkennung; *im Plural*: Danksagung
help	Hilfe
assistance	Assistenz, Unterstützung, Beistand
advice	Rat
to thank s.o.	jmdm. danken
to be grateful	dankbar sein
to acknowledge	würdigen, anerkennen
to fund	(finanziell) unterstützen, bezuschussen
support	Unterstützung
to support	unterstützen

Aufbauvokabular und Satzbeispiele

to thank s.o. **help**	The authors **thank** … for their **help** on cluster analysis.	jmdm. danken Hilfe
support	The authors **thank** the staff of the Cyclotron Unit for their interest and **support**, especially the radiographers for their invaluable technical **assistance**.	Unterstützung
assistance	We **thank** Ralph Stanton for his excellent technical **assistance**. We **thank** Jill Herrera for her administrative **assistance**.	Assistenz, Unterstützung, Beistand

to be grateful **advice**	The authors **are grateful** to … for **advice** and **support** in performing these studies.	dankbar sein Rat
to acknowledge	The authors gratefully **acknowledge** Petra Huber and … for their **help** with the bone scintigraphy quantifications; Matthias Plevic for his **support** with data collection; and all involved physicians, nurses, technicians, and members of the Department of Nuclear Medicine. The **assistance** of the Nuclear Medicine staff in acquiring data is gratefully **acknowledged**.	würdigen, anerkennen
acknowledge-ment *(BE)/* **acknowledgment** *(AE)*	Our special **acknowledgement** *(BE)/* **acknowledgment** *(AE)* is due to Tom Decker at TCU.	Anerkennung; *im Plural:* Danksagung
to address thanks to s.o.	The authors **address** special **thanks to** …	jmdm. danken, Dank an jmdn. richten
to extend thanks to s.o.	We wish to **extend** special **thanks to** …	jmdm. danken, Dank an jmdn. richten
to express grati-tude to s.o.	We also **express gratitude to** ..	jmdm. gegenüber Dank-barkeit zum Ausdruck bringen
to owe gratitude to s.o.	We **owe** sincere **gratitude to** Harry Miller Trevis, clinical director at …	jmdm. Dank schulden
to record one's gratitude to s.o.	The authors wish to **record their gratitude to** the clinical staff at Heidelberg University.	seinen Dank gegenüber jmdm. zum Ausdruck bringen
to show appre-ciation to s.o.	The authors also **show appreciation to** the doctors in the Department of Cardiology (Sunhill Medical Centre).	jmdn. dankend erwähnen (*wörtlich:* Wertschätzung ausdrücken)
Thanks are due to s.o.	**Thanks are** also **due to** Ella Lindberg …	Dank gebührt jmdm.

I. F Danksagungen

to be indebted to s.o. for s.th.	The authors **are** deeply **indebted to** the late Professor Billinggate **for** his unyielding **support** over a period of 23 years.	bei jmdm. in der Schuld stehen, jmdm. zu Dank verpflichtet sein
to fund	This study was **funded** by … This study was **funded** in part by grants from the National Institute of … This research was **funded** by the European Commission Research Project …	(finanziell) unterstützen, bezuschussen
to subsidize	This subject has been **subsidized** by the Whitechapel Research Society.	bezuschussen
to support	This research was **supported** in part by … This work was **supported** by a grant from the University of …	unterstützen

Vorträge
Oral presentation

1. Vorsitz und Moderation / Chairmanship

Words of welcome & Introduction of the chairpersons	Begrüßungsfloskeln & Vorstellen der Vorsitzenden
Ladies and gentlemen, welcome to the annual meeting of the European Association of …	Meine Damen und Herren, willkommen zur Jahrestagung der Europäischen Gesellschaft für …
Welcome to the session on …	Willkommen zur Session über …
Dear colleagues, welcome to the session on …	Liebe/Verehrte Kollegen, willkommen zur Session über …
Welcome to this afternoon session!	Willkommen zur Nachmittagssession!
Good morning, ladies and gentlemen. I am pleased to announce the session on …	Guten Morgen, meine Damen und Herren. Ich freue mich, Ihnen die Session über … ankündigen zu dürfen.
Good evening, ladies and gentlemen, we continue with the lecture on …	Guten Abend, meine Damen und Herren, wir fahren fort mit dem Vortrag/der Vorlesung über …
Let me introduce myself. I am Dr Rogers from the Department of Reconstructive Surgery at Liverpool University.	Ich darf mich vorstellen. Mein Name ist Dr. Rogers von der Fakultät für plastische Chirurgie an der Universität Liverpool.
It is a great honour for me to chair this first session on … My name is … from …	Es ist mir eine große Ehre, den Vorsitz über diese erste Session zum Thema … zu haben. Mein Name ist … und ich komme von/aus …
Good morning, everybody. My name is Gordon Green. Please welcome Dr Joan Ford from the University of Skirren. We will guide you through … and we will start straight away with the lecture of … from … on …	Guten Morgen zusammen. Ich heiße Gordon Green. Bitte begrüßen Sie Dr. Joan Ford von der Universität Skirren. Wir werden Sie durch … führen/begleiten und wir beginnen unverzüglich mit dem Vortrag von … aus/von … über …

II. 1. Vorsitz und Moderation

Good morning, ladies and gentlemen. Welcome to the session on molecular imaging in dementia. I am Dr Smith from Bristol Medical College. My co-chair for the first half of the session is Dr Taylor from Boston University.

Guten Morgen, meine Damen und Herren. Willkommen zur Session über molekulare Bildgebung bei Demenzen. Mein Name ist Dr. Smith vom Bristol Medical College. Den Vorsitz für die erste Hälfte der Session wird Dr. Taylor von der Universität Boston zusammen mit mir übernehmen.

I will co-chair this session with Professor Dalton.

Ich werde die Leitung der Session zusammen mit Professor Dalton übernehmen.

Introducing the speakers and topics	Vorstellen der Referenten und Themen
The first speaker I'd like to announce is …	Der erste Vortragende, den ich ankündigen möchte, ist …
Now I'd like to introduce the second speaker.	Nun möchte ich Ihnen den zweiten Redner vorstellen.
Now, without further ado, let's introduce …	Lassen Sie mich nun ohne weitere Umschweife … vorstellen.
I'd like Mr Smith to take the floor.	Ich möchte gerne Herrn Smith das Wort erteilen.
I would like to call Mr Smith to the podium.	Ich möchte gerne Herrn Smith zum Podium bitten.
It's a great pleasure for me to introduce Mr Smith.	Es ist mir eine große Freude, Ihnen Herrn Smith vorstellen zu dürfen.
Mr Smith, I believe you are the expert in this field.	Herr Smith, ich glaube, Sie sind der Experte auf diesem Gebiet.
Mr Smith will report on the latest results of the ARIADNE study.	Herr Smith wird uns über die Ergebnisse der ARIADNE-Studie berichten.
Mr Smith, please.	Herr Smith, bitte.
It is my great pleasure to introduce Ms Taylor.	Ich freue mich, Ihnen Frau Taylor vorstellen zu dürfen.
It is a great honour for me to announce …	Es ist mir eine große Ehre, … ankündigen zu dürfen.

I am particularly proud to welcome Dr Merten, who is going to give us a presentation on …

Besonders stolz bin ich, Dr. Merten begrüßen zu dürfen. Er wird uns über … berichten.

It is really a pleasure to have you here, Dr Soames.

Ich freue mich sehr, Sie heute hier zu haben, Dr. Soames.

I'd also like to announce Jennifer Goulston.

Auch/Außerdem möchte ich Jennifer Goulston begrüßen/ankündigen.

Dr Merten is next, I believe. The title of his presentation is …

Dr. Merten ist wohl der Nächste. Der Titel seines Vortrages heißt …

I am very happy to welcome the next speaker, Ms Taylor, who has managed to fill in for Mr Smith at very short notice.

Ich bin sehr glücklich, die nächste Rednerin, Frau Taylor, willkommen zu heißen, die es geschafft hat, sehr kurzfristig für Herrn Smith einzuspringen.

The next speaker is Dr Smith with a presentation of …

Der nächste Vortragende ist Dr. Smith mit einer Präsentation über …

The next lecture is about …

Der nächste Vortrag geht über …

The title of the next presentation is …

Der Titel des nächsten Vortrages lautet …

We will proceed with the lecture on …

Wir fahren fort mit dem Vortrag über …

We move on to the last talk of this session.

Und weiter geht's mit dem letzten Vortrag dieser Session.

The last presentation of this session deals with …

Der letzte Vortrag dieser Session behandelt …

We now finish up this morning session with the lecture of Ms …

Wir beenden die Vormittags-Session mit dem Vortrag/der Vorlesung von Frau …

Thanking the speakers	Dank an den Vortragenden

Thank you very much for this interesting lecture on …

Vielen Dank für diesen interessanten Vortrag/diese interessante Vorlesung über …

Thank you for this (very/most) instructive lecture.

Danke für den (äußerst) aufschlussreichen/lehrreichen Vortrag.

II. 1. Vorsitz und Moderation

Thank you for this comprehensive overview.

Danke schön für diesen umfassenden Überblick.

Thank you, Ms Taylor, for your riveting contribution on the latest developments in …

Frau Taylor, danke für Ihren fesselnden Beitrag über die jüngsten Entwicklungen auf dem Gebiet der …

Dr Smith really provided an excellent survey.

Dr. Smith hat wirklich einen exzellenten Überblick präsentiert.

Richard has supplied a superb analysis of …

Richard hat eine fantastische Analyse des/der … abgeliefert.

Call for questions	Aufforderung zu Fragen

Are there any questions from the audience?

Gibt es Fragen aus dem Publikum?

Any questions or comments?

(Irgendwelche) Fragen oder Anmerkungen?

One or two quick questions before we proceed to the next session.

Ein, zwei schnelle Fragen, bevor wir zur nächsten Session kommen.

Weitere Varianten für die Eröffnung der Frage- und Diskussionsrunde finden Sie im Kapitel II. 8 „Aufforderung zu Fragen / How to invite the audience to ask questions".

Observing a timeframe	Im Zeitplan bleiben

Owing to our tight schedule I'd like to remind the speakers to keep an eye on the time.

Aufgrund unseres engen Programms möchte ich alle Vortragenden daran erinnern, auf die Zeit zu achten.

We have already fallen behind schedule. So I'd like to remind all speakers to observe the time limit.

Wir sind bereits hinter den Zeitplan zurück gefallen. Ich möchte deshalb alle Vortragenden daran erinnern, auf ihre Redezeiten zu achten.

We're running short of time.

Die Zeit wird knapp.

Unfortunately, we have stretched the time frame to its limit. I'll therefore have to ask Dr Smith to gradually come to the end of his presentation.	Unglücklicherweise haben wir unseren Zeitrahmen ausgereizt. Ich muss Dr. Smith deshalb bitten, allmählich zum Ende seiner Präsentation zu kommen.
I'm afraid we're running out of time. Dr Smith, will you please come to your conclusions?	Bedauerlicherweise neigt sich unsere Zeit dem Ende zu. Dr. Smith, würden Sie bitte zu Ihren Schlussfolgerungen kommen?
Dr Smith, you have exceeded your speech time. Would you please try and come to an end within the next minute or so?	Dr. Smith, Sie haben Ihre Redezeit überzogen. Würden Sie bitte versuchen, in Kürze zum Ende zu kommen?
We're doing well for time.	Wir liegen gut in der Zeit.

Announcing breaks	**Pausen ankündigen**
We'll take a short break and resume at twelve-thirty.	Wir machen eine kurze Pause und fahren um zwölf Uhr dreißig fort.
I suggest we take a ten-minute break.	Ich schlage vor, wir machen zehn Minuten Pause.
Let's take a short break, shall we?	Machen wir eine kurze Pause.
We're coming up to our first fifteen-minute break. I see you all again at 13.15.	Es ist Zeit für unsere erste fünfzehnminütige Pause. Wir sehen uns alle um 13 Uhr 15 wieder.
Our lunch break is coming up shortly. Please make sure to be back in time for the afternoon session, which is scheduled to start at 2 pm.	In Kürze ist Mittagspause. Bitte seien Sie pünktlich zur Nachmittagssession wieder zurück, die um 14 Uhr beginnt.
We're taking a ten-minute recess now.	Wir unterbrechen für 10 Minuten. *(förmlich; auch bei Gerichtsverhandlungen)*
I now declare this session in recess until 9 am tomorrow.	Ich vertage diese Sitzung hiermit auf morgen früh, 9 Uhr.

II. 1. Vorsitz und Moderation

Closing the session	Schlussworte
It has been a most instructive and rewarding session. Thanks to all the speakers for their contributions.	Die heutige Session war sehr lehrreich und hat uns allen etwas gebracht. Ich danke allen Vortragenden für ihre Beiträge.
We have now reached the end of this session. I would like to thank the speakers for their excellent presentations. Thanks also to the audience for joining us.	Wir sind am Ende der Session angekommen. Ich möchte den Vortragenden für ihre exzellenten Präsentationen danken. Danke auch an das Publikum für die Teilnahme.
We've come to the end of the session. Let me thank all of you for making this symposium such a memorable event. I'm looking forward to the evening session on … which starts at 18.00 hours.	Wir sind am Ende der Session angelangt. Lassen Sie mich Ihnen allen dafür danken, dass dieses Symposium so ein beeindruckendes (*wörtlich*: denkwürdiges) Ereignis wurde. Ich freue mich auf die Abendsitzung zum Thema …, die um 18 Uhr beginnt.

Miscellaneous	Verschiedenes
Please take a seat.	Bitte nehmen Sie Platz.
There are still some seats available in the front rows.	In den vorderen Reihen sind noch Plätze frei.
Dr Smith, please speak up as some people in the back cannot hear you.	Dr. Smith, sprechen Sie bitte etwas lauter, da man Sie in den hinteren Reihen nicht hören kann.
Please make sure that your mobile phone is switched off.	Bitte denken Sie daran, Ihre Handys auszuschalten.

2. Einleitung / Introduction

Polite opening	Eröffnungsfloskeln
Thank you, Mr Chairman.	Danke, Herr Vorsitzender.
Madam Chairman, thank you for the opportunity to talk about … tonight.	Frau Vorsitzende, ich danke Ihnen für die Gelegenheit, heute Abend über … zu sprechen.
Good morning, ladies and gentlemen, and thank you for inviting me to talk to you today.	Guten Morgen, meine Damen und Herren, und danke, dass Sie mich eingeladen haben, um heute zu Ihnen zu sprechen.
Thanks for having me here tonight.	Danke, dass ich heute Abend hier sein darf.
Thank you very much for inviting me.	Vielen Dank, dass Sie mich eingeladen haben.
It's a great pleasure for me to follow this invitation.	Es ist mir eine große Freude, dieser Einladung zu folgen.
I feel honoured to speak here today.	Es ist mir eine Ehre, heute hier zu sprechen.
I'd like to thank the organizers for inviting me.	Ich bedanke mich bei den Organisatoren für die Einladung.
I'd like to thank the organizers for giving me the honour to talk here.	Ich möchte mich gerne bei den Organisatoren dafür bedanken, dass Sie mir die Ehre erwiesen haben, hier sprechen zu dürfen.
Thank you for the introduction and the invitation to speak here.	Ich danke Ihnen für die einführenden Worte und die Einladung hier zu sprechen.

Topic and aim of the lecture	Thema und Ziel des Vortrags
This lecture is about …	In diesem Vortrag/dieser Vorlesung geht es um …
This session is on …	Dieser Vortrag/diese Vorlesung/diese Session behandelt/befasst sich mit …

II. 2. Einleitung

My topic today is …	Heute spreche ich über …
The title of this talk is …	Das Thema meines Vortrags lautet …
My talk is mainly concerned with …	Mein Vortrag beschäftigt sich hauptsächlich mit …
My talk is chiefly about …	In meinem Vortrag geht es hauptsächlich um …
In this lecture, I'm going to report …	In diesem Vortrag/dieser Vorlesung werde ich über … berichten.
In this lecture, I'm going to present the results of …	In diesem Vortrag/dieser Vorlesung werde ich die Ergebnisse von … vorstellen.
What I'm going to present is …	Was ich (Ihnen) vorstellen/zeigen möchte, ist …
What we're going to do in the next hour is …	In der nächsten Stunde werden wir …
So this is what we are going to do: …	Wir werden Folgendes machen: …
The purpose of this presentation is …	Zweck dieses Vortrags ist es, …
My presentation mainly deals with …	Ich referiere im Wesentlichen über …
During the next few minutes, I'd like to …	In den nächsten Minuten möchte ich …
The aim of my lecture is …	Das Ziel meines Vortrags ist …
The objective is to …	Ziel ist es, …
I'd like to focus on …	Ich möchte mich auf … konzentrieren.

Structure of the lecture	Gliederung des Vortrags
First of all, a word on …	Zunächst (einmal) ein paar Worte über …
Before we start, I'd like to …	Bevor es los geht, möchte ich …
Let's start/begin with …	Lassen Sie uns mit … beginnen.

To start with, I'll give you an overview of ... | Zu Beginn/Als Einstieg möchte ich Ihnen einen Überblick über ... geben.

Let us first look at an overview of my lecture. | Betrachten wir zunächst die Gliederung meines Vortrags.

I'd like to give you a broad outline of ... | Ich möchte Ihnen einen groben Überblick geben über ...

Let me give you a quick rundown on ... | Ich möchte Sie kurz über ... informieren.

To start, I want to show you ... | Zu Beginn/Als Einstieg möchte ich Ihnen ... zeigen.

Let us first talk about ... | Sprechen wir zunächst über ...

I'd like to touch upon ... | Ich möchte kurz auf ... eingehen.

In the first ten minutes I am going to give you a short overview of ... | In den nächsten zehn Minuten gebe ich Ihnen einen kurzen Überblick über ...

In the 20 minutes to come I will give you an overview of ... | In den kommenden zwanzig Minuten werde ich Ihnen einen Überblick geben über ...

I'd like to spend the first couple of minutes talking about the challenges of O&G. | Zunächst einmal möchte ich kurz auf die Herausforderungen in der Geburtshilfe und Gynäkologie eingehen.

Our goals are first, to review the basic principles of ... | Unsere Ziele bestehen zunächst darin, die grundlegenden Prinzipien von ... näher zu betrachten.

After a brief introduction I will focus on ... | Nach einer kurzen Einführung werde ich mich auf ... konzentrieren.

Then I am/we are going to talk about ... | Dann/danach werde ich/werden wir über ... sprechen.

The topics we are going to talk about are ... | Die Themen, über die wir sprechen werden, sind ...

I'm going to divide this presentation into three parts. | Ich werde meinen Vortrag in drei Abschnitte gliedern/unterteilen.

And then we will spend about half an hour discussing the cases. | Und dann widmen wir etwa eine halbe Stunde den Fällen.

II. 2. Einleitung

As we go along we shall discuss various aspects of …

Im (weiteren) Verlauf werden wir verschiedene Gesichtspunkte von … ansprechen.

At last, I would like to …

Zum Schluss würde ich gerne …

We will finish with …

Wir werden mit … schließen.

And finally, we are taking a closer look at …

Und am Ende beschäftigen wir uns näher mit …

3. Überleitungen / How to link up passages

Moving on	Weiter geht's
That's it for the introduction. Now …	Soviel zur Einleitung. Jetzt …
Now let's take a look at …	Lassen Sie uns nun … betrachten.
Now we move on to …	Wir kommen nun zu …
	Wir machen weiter mit …
Moving on now to …	Weiter geht es mit …
That brings me to …	Das führt mich zu …
The next issue I shall concentrate on is …	Das nächste Thema, auf das ich mich konzentrieren werde, ist …
The next issue I'd like to focus on is …	Das nächste Thema, auf das ich mich konzentrieren werde, ist …
Let me come to my second topic.	Ich komme zum zweiten Thema.
This is another …	Das ist ein weiteres/ein weiterer/eine weitere …
This is another interesting aspect which leads me to …	Dies ist ein weiterer interessanter Aspekt, der mich zu … führt.
May I turn to another aspect of …?	Darf ich mich einem anderen Aspekt von … zuwenden?
Let's go through this topic quickly.	Lassen Sie mich dieses Thema rasch abhandeln.
I should like to quickly run you through this intriguing subject.	Ich möchte Ihnen dieses faszinierende Thema gerne kurz vorstellen.
(Is) Everybody with me so far?	Können Sie mir soweit folgen?
Before we proceed, we must consider …	Bevor wir fortfahren, müssen wir … bedenken.

II. 3. Überleitungen

Just a few comments I'd like to make before …

Lassen Sie mich nur ein paar Anmerkungen machen, bevor …

I'd like to proceed with some examples of …

Ich möchte mit einigen Beispielen für … fortfahren.

Now that I have shown you …, we proceed with …

Nachdem ich (Ihnen) jetzt … gezeigt habe, fahren wir fort mit …

We had better move on as we are rather pushed for time.

Wir fahren besser fort, da wir wenig Zeit haben.

Changing the subject	Themawechsel

Let me broach another subject/problem/question.

Lassen Sie mich ein weiteres Thema/Problem/eine weitere Frage ansprechen.

I would now like to briefly broach the subject of …

Ich möchte jetzt gerne kurz das Thema … anschneiden.

I am going to turn, if I may, to another issue.

Ich wende mich nun, wenn Sie gestatten, einem anderen Thema zu.

I want to take a moment to talk about …

Ich möchte kurz auf … eingehen.

Now I want to take a few minutes to talk about …

Nun möchte ich ein paar Minuten auf … verwenden.

I want to spend a minute or two on …

Ich möchte ein, zwei Minuten über … reden.

Now let us briefly turn to … in the time we have left.

Lassen Sie uns in der verbleibenden Zeit kurz auf … eingehen.

Just a word or two about …

Nur ein, zwei Sätze zu …

Let me make a few remarks on …

Ich möchte ein paar Dinge zu … sagen.

Let's deal with …

Ich behandle nun …

We'll talk about that in a second.

Dazu kommen wir gleich.

We'll come to that later.

Dazu kommen wir später.

Let us now discuss the pros and cons of ...	Sprechen wir nun über das Pro und Kontra vor ...
Let us quickly weigh/evaluate the pros and cons ...	Wenn wir rasch Pro und Kontra gegeneinander abwägen, ...
And another interesting feature needs mentioning, namely ...	Auch sollte ein weiteres interessantes Merkmal Erwähnung finden, nämlich ...
The following aspect needs to be mentioned as well.	Der folgende Gesichtspunkt muss ebenfalls erwähnt werden.
I am now moving on to item number 14 in my presentation.	Weiter geht es mit Punkt 14 meines Vortrages.
Allow me to bring you up to date now.	Ich möchte Sie nun auf den aktuellen Stand bringen.
Let me digress for a moment ...	Lassen Sie mich einen Augenblick abschweifen ...
If I may digress for a moment ...	Wenn ich kurz abschweifen darf, ...
Another point to be mentioned in any discussion of this problem/issue, is ...	Was in jeder Diskussion dieses Problems/ Themas erwähnt werden muss, ist folgender Punkt: ...
Where does that lead us?	Was bringt uns das?
	Wo befinden wir uns jetzt?

> **INFO:** *Nachstehend finden Sie universell verwendbare Überleitungspartikel, ohne sinntragende Übersetzung, an die sich jegliche Art der Äußerung anschließen kann.*

So ...

Now ...

Anyway ...

II. 3. Überleitungen

Anyhow …

Right …

Well …

Moving back	Nochmal zurück
But back to …	Doch zurück zu …
Now we come back to …	Wir kommen nun zurück zu …
Let us just take one moment to revisit …	Lassen Sie uns einen Augenblick zu … zurückkehren.
Let's go back to my introductory remarks on …	Lassen Sie uns (kurz) auf meine einführenden Bemerkungen zurückkommen.
I'd like to return to what I said earlier on.	Ich würde gerne noch einmal auf das zurückkommen, was ich vorher gesagt habe.
I've mentioned to you before that …	Ich erwähnte zuvor, dass …
There's one thing I forgot to tell you.	Eine Sache habe ich vergessen zu erwähnen.
Coming back to what I've just said *(BE)*/ Coming back to what I just said *(AE)* …	Um auf das zurückzukommen, was ich gerade/soeben gesagt habe, …
At the risk of repeating myself, …	Auf die Gefahr hin, mich zu wiederholen, …
Even at the risk of repeating myself …	Auch auf die Gefahr hin, dass ich mich wiederhole, …
I almost forgot …	Fast hätte ich … vergessen.
Can I backtrack for just a second here?	Können wir kurz noch mal zurück? Kann ich das kurz noch mal in Erinnerung rufen?
Let's pick up on one of the points that were raised before the break.	Lassen Sie mich einen der Punkte aufgreifen, die vor der Pause angeschnitten wurden.

As we are doing well for time, I suggest we quite briefly take stock of what we have covered so far.

Da wir gut in der Zeit liegen, schlage ich vor, wir ziehen eine kleine Zwischenbilanz dessen, was wir bisher angesprochen haben.

End in sight	Zum Schluss kommen
Finally, I want to talk about …	Zum Schluss möchte ich (noch) über … sprechen.
Finally, a word on …	Zum Abschluss ein paar Worte zu …
This is going to be my last topic.	Kommen wir nun zu meinem letzten Thema.
We are going to move on to our penultimate/last topic.	Wir kommen nun zu unserem vorletzten/letzten Thema.
In the last five minutes we will talk about …	In den letzten fünf Minuten sprechen wir über …
I'd like to spend the remaining time on …	Den Rest der Zeit würde ich gerne mit … verbringen.
	Die verbleibende Zeit würde ich gerne … widmen/über … sprechen.
For the rest of the time, let me address …	Lassen Sie mich in der verbleibenden Zeit … ansprechen.
Before finishing, I want to show you …	Bevor ich zum Ende komme, möchte ich Ihnen … zeigen.
(Just) Two more slides.	(Nur) Noch zwei Folien/Dias.
My presentation is drawing to its end.	Ich bin gleich mit meinem Vortrag fertig.
We are almost finished.	Wir sind fast fertig.
If you will bear with me, I won't be keeping you long.	Wenn Sie mir noch kurz Gehör schenken wollen; ich bin fast fertig. / Sie haben es gleich geschafft.
Let me close with the words …	Lassen Sie mich mit den Worten schließen: …

125

II. 3. Überleitungen

One final remark ...

Noch eine abschließende Bemerkung: ...

I would like to conclude my comments by saying that ...

Ich möchte meine Ausführungen gerne schließen und sagen, dass ...

Let's begin the discussion with ...

Beginnen wir die Diskussion mit . .

4. Dias, Folien und grafische Elemente / Slides, transparencies and graphics

Slide projection	Diaprojektion

INFO: *Je nachdem, welches Medium Sie benutzen, heißt* **slide** *entweder Dia oder (Präsentations-)Folie.*

Could I have the first slide, please?	Könnte ich bitte das erste Dia haben?
First slide, please.	Das erste Dia bitte.
Next slide, please.	Nächstes Dia bitte.
We have just skipped a slide there.	Wir haben ein Dia übersprungen.
Could you go back one slide, please?	Könnten Sie bitte ein Dia zurückgehen?
Back one more, please.	Noch eins (zurück), bitte.
Could I have the one before, please?	Könnte ich das vorherige (Dia) haben, bitte?
Could we go back to the very first slide again, please?	Könnten wir bitte das allererste Dia noch ma haben?
We need to go back to the second slide.	Wir müssen zum zweiten Dia zurück.
May I just go back to the last slide?	Wenn ich noch einmal zum letzten Dia zurück darf …
I'm afraid the slide you see is not quite up to date.	Leider ist das Dia, das Sie hier sehen, nicht ganz auf dem aktuellen Stand.

What you see	Was man sieht
The first slide shows you …	Das erste Dia zeigt Ihnen …
The second/next slide shows you …	Das zweite/nächste Dia zeigt Ihnen …
On the next slide you can see …	Auf dem nächsten Dia können Sie … sehen.

127

II. 4. Dias, Folien und grafische Elemente

Here you can see …	Hier sehen Sie …
What you can also see is …	Was Sie auch sehen können, ist …
We are looking at …	Wir schauen auf …
	Wir sehen hier …
What we're looking at here is …	Was wir hier sehen, ist …
These images show …	Diese Bilder/Abbildungen zeigen _.
The following chart might help illustrate this point.	Das folgende Schaubild hilft vielleicht, diesen Punkt zu veranschaulichen.
Have a look at the next graph, please.	Sehen Sie sich bitte die folgende Kurve/ Funktion an.
The diagram on the right demonstrates …	Das rechte Diagramm zeigt/demonstriert …
Why don't you check the following chart against your handouts?	Vergleichen Sie doch einmal die folgende Tabelle mit Ihrem Handout.
The next transparency highlights …	Die nächste Folie beleuchtet … näher.
This slide looks very busy.	Dieses Dia sieht ziemlich überfrachtet/ unübersichtlich aus.
This number should read 4.0 instead of 40%.	Das soll 4,0 statt 40 % heißen.
This number ought to read 4.0 instead of 40%.	Das sollte eigentlich 4,0 statt 40 % heißen.
What you see in square brackets is in fact a typo; it should read TDI instead of TDP.	Was Sie in eckigen Klammern sehen, ist in Wirklichkeit ein Druckfehler; es sollte TDI heißen anstatt TDP.
This is quite obviously a misprint.	Hier handelt es sich ganz offensichtlich um einen Druckfehler.
I am sorry. This should be an "N" rather than a "T".	Tut mir leid. Das sollte ein „N" sein und kein „T".

What do these symbols denote?	Was bezeichnen nun diese Symbole?
Quantities are all in millilitres unless otherwise stated.	Die Mengenangaben sind alle in Millilitern, sofern nicht anders angegeben.

Guiding the audience	Aufmerksamkeit lenken
Let's take a look at …	Werfen wir einen Blick auf …
	Sehen wir uns … an.
I want to draw your attention to …	Ich möchte Ihre Aufmerksamkeit gerne auf … lenken.
May I draw your attention to …?	Darf ich Ihre Aufmerksamkeit auf … lenken?
If I may/might draw your attention to …	Wenn ich Ihre Aufmerksamkeit auf … lenken darf/dürfte.
Please close your attention on …	Bitte richten Sie Ihre Aufmerksamkeit auf …
I call your attention to …	Richten Sie Ihre Aufmerksamkeit auf …
Please pay attention to …	Bitte richten Sie Ihre Aufmerksamkeit auf …
I would like you to pay special attention to …	Beachten Sie bitte vor allem …
You can see that this chapter is headed "…"	Wie Sie sehen können, heißt dieses Kapitel „…"
This is probably the most important slide of the entire presentation.	Dies ist vermutlich das wichtigste Dia der gesamten Präsentation.
(Please) Note that …	Beachten Sie (bitte), dass …
Notice that …	Nehmen Sie zur Kenntnis, dass …
You ought to focus on …	Sie sollten Ihr Augenmerk auf … richten.
at the top/bottom	oben/unten
on the right/left	rechts/links

II. 4. Dias, Folien und grafische Elemente

in the middle/centre

in der Mitte

At the head of the list you can see …

Zu Beginn der Aufstellung sehen Sie …

The upper part of the diagram shows …

Der obere Teil des Diagramms zeigt …

Please look at the lower right-hand corner of the slide.

Bitte betrachten Sie die rechte untere Ecke des Dias.

Giving examples	Beispiele anführen

Here is an example of …

Hier ist ein Beispiel für …

Let me show you one example of …

Lassen Sie mich Ihnen ein Beispiel für … zeigen.

I have got another example.

Ich habe ein weiteres Beispiel.

Yet another example of … is …

Und noch ein weiteres Beispiel für … ist …

A good example of this is …

Ein gutes Beispiel hierfür ist …

To illustrate that point I'd like to show you …

Um dies zu veranschaulichen, möchte ich Ihnen … zeigen.

These are my co-workers: …

Dies sind meine Co-Autoren: …

(Wenn am Ende des Vortrags ein Dia mit den Namen des Forschungsteams ge- zeigt wird.)

Technical aspects and problems	Technische Fragen und Probleme

I believe there is something wrong with the microphone/mike.

Ich glaube, irgendetwas stimmt nicht mit dem Mikrofon/Mikro.

Can you all hear me without the micro- phone/mike?

Kann mich jeder hören ohne Mikrofon/ Mikro?

Can the people in the back hear me clearly?

Können Sie mich da hinten gut verstehen?

The microphone should transfer over, but it doesn't.

Das Mikrofon ist (noch) nicht umgeschaltet.

(Wenn Sie einen anderen Platz auf dem Podium einnehmen und die Technik nicht umschaltet.)

Looks like we are having some technical problem.

Sieht aus, als hätten wir hier ein technisches Problem.

What's going on?

Was ist da los?

What's wrong with this pointer?

Was stimmt mit diesem Pointer nicht?

I'm afraid this pointer is not working (properly).

Ich fürchte, dieser Pointer funktioniert nicht (richtig).

Which of you knows his/her/their way around that pointer?

Wer von Ihnen kennt sich mit dem Pointer hier aus?

Funny gadget.

Komisches Gerät.

Is there another power point/socket?

Gibt es noch eine Steckdose?

This is not the slide I wanted.

Das ist nicht das Dia, das ich wollte.

Be forewarned – the reproduction is not very good on the screen.

Ich möchte Sie vorwarnen – die Abbildung kommt in der Projektion nicht besonders gut (zur Geltung).

I'm very sorry – this screen/image has just frozen!

Es tut mir sehr leid – diese Ansicht/dieses Bild hat sich soeben aufgehängt.

The animation/video clip is not running properly. Let me describe what you should be seeing rather than hearing right now.

Die Animation/Das Video läuft nicht einwandfrei. Lassen Sie mich beschreiben, was Sie jetzt eigentlich sehen sollten, anstatt es von mir zu hören.

The programme *(BE)*/program *(AE)* has stalled again – it beats/beggars belief!

Das Programm ist schon wieder stehen geblieben – ich kann es nicht glauben!

That's not part of the presentation.

Das gehört nicht zum Vortrag.

Looks as if we cannot proceed.

Sieht nicht so aus, als könnten wir fortfahren.

Well, I do apologize for the delay.

Ich muss mich für die Verzögerung entschuldigen.

II. 4. Dias, Folien und grafische Elemente

We are getting a technician to look into it. That shouldn't take long. Please remain seated.

Ein Techniker wird sich darum kümmern. Das sollte nicht lange dauern. Bitte bleiben Sie auf Ihren Plätzen.

Bear with me a minute, ladies and gentlemen; it shouldn't take long to sort out this technical problem.

Gedulden Sie sich bitte einen Augenblick, meine Damen und Herren; wir solten dieses technische Problem rasch in den Griff bekommen.

Could you please turn the lights on?

Könnten Sie bitte das Licht einschalten?

Could you please dim the lights a bit?

Könnten Sie bitte das Licht etwas runterdrehen?

Could we have the main lights down, please?

Könnte jemand bitte das Licht ausmachen?

There appears to be some problem with the lights.

Anscheinend haben wir ein Problem mit dem Licht.

Why don't we all grab some coffee until the technical problems are sorted?

Warum holen wir uns nicht einfach einen Kaffee, bis die technischen Probleme behoben sind?

5. Hervorhebungen / How to emphasize

I want to emphasize (to you) that …   Ich möchte (Ihnen gegenüber) betonen, dass …

We have to emphasize that …   Man muss betonen, dass …

Let me emphasize once again the crucial role of this model.   Lassen Sie mich noch einmal auf die Schlüsselrolle dieses Modells hinweisen.

Lassen Sie mich noch einmal betonen, welch entscheidende Rolle dieses Modell spielt.

I'd like to put the emphasis on …   Ich möchte den Schwerpunkt/die Betonung auf … legen.

I'd like to stress again that …   Ich möchte noch einmal betonen, dass …

I'd like to point out that …   Ich möchte darauf hinweisen, dass …

Keep in mind that …   Denken Sie daran, dass …

Merken Sie sich, dass …

Commit this to your memory, please!   Merken Sie sich das bitte!

(Keine Rüge, sondern Aufforderung, etw. im Gedächtnis zu behalten.)

What is important?   Was ist wichtig?

(Sie geben selbst gleich die Antwort.)

What is important is …   Was wichtig ist, ist …

What is most important is that …   Was am wichtigsten ist, ist …

The important thing is …   Wichtig ist …

That's a very important finding.   Das ist eine sehr wichtige Beobachtung/Feststellung.

Here is one important point I'd like to make.   Einen Punkt möchte ich besonders hervorheben.

II. 5. Hervorhebungen

This is especially important to the audience here.

Dies ist von besonderer Bedeutung für unser Publikum.

… is paramount.

… ist von herausragender Bedeutung.

You have to be aware of (yet) another important aspect, namely …

Sie müssen sich (noch) einen weiteren wichtigen Aspekt vor Augen führen, nämlich …

There is (yet) another important feature that I want you to be aware of: …

Ich möchte, dass Sie sich noch einen anderen/weiteren wichtigen Aspekt vor Augen führen: …

That is a definite plus!

Das ist definitiv ein Pluspunkt/Vorteil.

I want you to recognize that …

Ich möchte, dass Sie erkennen/anerkennen, dass …

What matters (most) is (the fact) that …

Worauf es (am meisten) ankommt, ist (die Tatsache), dass …

In this context it is nevertheless worthy of note that …

Gleichwohl ist es in diesem Zusammenhang erwähnenswert, dass …

This is indeed its most salient characteristic.

In der Tat ist dies das hervorstechendste Merkmal von …

Let me draw/call/direct your attention to the following point …

Richten Sie Ihr Augenmerk auf folgenden Punkt …

One of the issues to underscore is …

Eines der Themen, die man unterstreichen muss, ist …

One of the key issues is …

Eines der entscheidenden Themen ist …

… but the key point is …

… doch der zentrale Punkt ist …

The main point here is …

Das Wichtigste ist …

The point I want to make today is …

Was ich Ihnen heute mitgeben möchte, ist …

Worauf ich heute hinaus will, ist …

Let me be explicit on that point.

Ich möchte dies unmissverständlich zum Ausdruck bringen.

This is what I want to say!

Darum geht es mir!

Das ist es, worauf ich hinaus will!

I want to really concentrate on ... because we have limited time.

Ich möchte mich eigentlich auf ... konzentrieren, da unsere Zeit begrenzt ist.

These findings are the icing on the cake.

Diese Ergebnisse sind das I-Tüpfelchen.

6. Bezug nehmen auf andere Redner / Referring to other speakers

Let me, briefly, come back to what Dr Richardson has said.

Lassen Sie mich rasch auf das zurückkommen, was Dr. Richardson gesagt hat.

You have already heard from various speakers this morning, and in particular from Professor Folcrum, that the unusually high boiling points for … result from …

Wie Sie bereits von mehreren Vortragenden heute Morgen gehört haben, insbesondere von Prof. Folcrum, haben die ungewöhnlich hohen Siedepunkte von … ihre Ursache in …

Professor Stilton puts it this way: "…".

Prof. Stilton formuliert es so: „…".

According to my esteemed colleague Jane Witherspoon, the effects are …

Meiner geschätzten Kollegin Jane Witherspoon zufolge sind die Auswirkungen …

According to Martin Anglim, a biological sciences professor at Columbia University, the conclusions drawn by you, Dr Tilly, need modifying. In physics there are several …

Martin Anglim zufolge, (einem) Professor für Biowissenschaften an der Columbia-Universität, müssen Ihre Schlussfolgerungen modifiziert werden, Dr. Tilly. In der Physik gibt es etliche …

What I have just said applies equally to Dr Patterson's theory.

Was ich soeben gesagt habe, gilt gleichermaßen für die Theorie von Dr. Patterson.

Dr Soames has done a fine job filling us all in on the tangible side-effects of Orbit-Pro-1A.

Dr. Soames hat hervorragende Arbeit geleistet, als er uns über die handfesten Nebenwirkungen von OrbitPro-1A unterrichtet hat.

When tackling the hairy subject of … we must, first, follow up on Dr Jameson's results.

Wollen wir das delikate Thema … ansprechen, so müssen wir zunächst an Dr. Jamesons Ergebnisse anknüpfen.

I should like to link with the topic discussed by Professor Waugh last night.

Ich möchte gerne an das Thema von Prof. Waugh anknüpfen, das er gestern Abend behandelt hat.

7. Zusammenfassung/Schlusswort / Summary/Closing Remarks

Summary	Zusammenfassung
All in all, …	Alles in allem …
All things considered …	Alles in allem …
In one word, …	Mit einem Wort …/ Kurzum …
Summing up, …	Zusammenfassend …
To sum up, …	Zusammenfassend …
To summarize …	Zusammenfassend …
In summary, what I have tried to show you is …	Um zusammenzufassen: Was ich versucht habe, Ihnen zu zeigen …
Let's summarize briefly what we've been looking at so far …	Lassen Sie uns kurz zusammenfassen, was wir bisher behandelt haben …
Let me summarize the aforementioned results in one simple phrase.	Lassen Sie mich die bisher genannten Ergebnisse auf eine Formel bringen/in einem einfachen Satz zusammenfassen.
Taking everything into account/consideration, …	Wenn man all das/alles berücksichtigt, …
What's the upshot of all this?	Was ist das Fazit/Ergebnis des Ganzen?
It is safe to say …	Wir können mit Sicherheit sagen, …

Closing remarks	Schlusswort
To conclude, I would like to …	Abschließend würde ich gerne …
In conclusion we may say that …	Abschließend kann man sagen, dass …
The conclusion of this lecture is …	Wir folgern aus meinem Vortrag …
	Die Schlussfolgerung meiner Vorlesung ist …

II. 7. Zusammenfassung/Schlusswort

Let me conclude …	Lassen Sie mich abschließen …
So let me come to my conclusions here.	Lassen Sie mich also zu meinen Schlussfolgerungen kommen.
With those remarks, I'd like to conclude …	Mit diesen Anmerkungen möchte ich (ab)schließen …
Let me just make one final remark.	Lassen Sie mich noch eine letzte Bemerkung machen.
I would like to make one final remark, if you please.	Wenn Sie mich freundlicherweise eine letzte Anmerkung machen ließen.
I'd like to round off by saying …	Ich würde gerne schließen mit den Worten …
Just a couple of very quick points.	Noch rasch ein paar kurze Punkte
Finally, I'd like to remind you of two of the issues we have covered …	Abschließend möchte ich zwei der behandelten Themen in Erinnerung rufen …
One thing before you leave: …	Eine Sache noch, bevor Sie gehen: …
I'd like to finish now by sharing this impressive chart with you.	Mit diesem beeindruckenden Diagramm möchte ich nun schließen.
	Ich möchte nun zum Abschluss kommen und Ihnen diese beeindruckende Tabelle/ dieses beeindruckende Schaubild mit auf den Weg geben.
With that I finish my lecture.	Hiermit beende ich meine Vorlesung.
Well, that's it!	Das war's!

Take-home message	Kernaussage
So what the study has shown is …	Was die Studie also gezeigt hat, ist …
What I want you to take home is …	Was Sie mit nach Hause nehmen sollen, ist …
The take-home message (here) is …	Die „Take-Home-Message" ist …

The take-home points are …	Was Sie mit nach Hause nehmen sollen, ist …
The gist of this study is as follows: …	Das Wesentliche dieser Studie lautet wie folgt: …
The bottom line of this survey is …	Die Kernaussage dieser Studie lautet …
This is my chief concern: …	Dies ist mein Hauptanliegen: …

Thanking the audience	**Dank an das Publikum**
Thank you.	Danke schön.
Thank you/Thanks for your attention.	Danke für Ihre Aufmerksamkeit.
Thank you very much indeed.	Vielen, vielen Dank.
Thanks very much indeed for coming!	Danke, dass Sie gekommen sind! Danke, dass Sie da waren!
I would like to thank everybody for being here today.	Ich danke Ihnen allen, dass Sie heute hier waren.
I want to thank everyone in this room.	Ich danke allen hier Anwesenden.
With that I will thank you for your attention.	Und damit danke ich Ihnen für Ihre Aufmerksamkeit.
That's all for now, thank you for having me.	Das wär's. Danke für die Einladung.
Thank you for your time, ladies and gentlemen.	Ich danke Ihnen (für Ihre Zeit), meine Damen und Herren.

Thanking others (if appropriate)	**Dank an andere (falls angebracht)**
I thank Rob Stilton for his excellent technical assistance.	Ich bedanke mich bei Rob Stilton für seine hervorragende Hilfe in technischen Dingen.
I am grateful to Professor Wharton for his advice and support.	Ich bin Professor Wharton dankbar für seinen Rat und seine Unterstützung.

II. 7. Zusammenfassung/Schlusswort

We gratefully acknowledge Gerard Dove for his help with data collection.

Dankbar erkennen wir die Hilfe von Gerard Dove bei der Datenerhebung an.

I should like to make acknowledgement *(BE)*/acknowledgment *(AE)* to ... for ...

Ich möchte mich gerne bei ... bedanken für ...

Thanks are (also) due to the Hillsborough trainees.

Dank gebührt (auch/ferner) den Praktikanten aus Hillsborough.

Let me extend special thanks to ...

Lassen Sie mich ganz besonders .. danken.

We wish to express gratitude to the organizers of this conference.

Wir möchten unsere Dankbarkeit gegenüber den Organisatoren dieser Konferenz zum Ausdruck bringen.

We show appreciation to the R&D staff at Whitfield.

Die Mitarbeiter der Forschungs- und Entwicklungsabteilung in Whitfield seien dankend erwähnt.

140

8. Aufforderung zu Fragen / How to invite the audience to ask questions

At the beginning of the lecture	Am Anfang des Vortrags
If you have any questions, I'll be glad to answer them at the end of my presentation.	Sollten Sie Fragen haben, so werde ich diese gerne am Ende meines Vortrages beantworten.
I should be grateful if you refrained from asking questions during my presentation as you will be given ample opportunity to do so later on.	Ich wäre Ihnen dankbar/sehr verbunden, wenn Sie sich mit Fragen während meines Vortrags zurückhalten würden; Sie werden an späterer Stelle hierzu reichlich Gelegenheit haben.
Perhaps you could hold back your questions until the end of my presentation, as we are going to have a question-and-answer session afterwards.	Vielleicht können Sie ja Ihre Fragen bis zum Ende meines Vortrags aufheben. Wir werden im Anschluss eine Frage- und Antwortrunde abhalten.
Let me run through the advantages of this model with you before taking questions.	Ich möchte gerne mit Ihnen die Vorteile dieses Modells durchsprechen und dann beantworte ich Ihre Fragen.
Please stop me any time you have a question.	Bitte stoppen Sie mich jederzeit, wenn Sie eine Frage haben.
I don't mind being interrupted if there is any question.	Sie dürfen mich gerne unterbrechen, wenn es Fragen gibt.
If there is any question to ask, please feel free to do so.	Wenn es irgendeine Frage gibt, fragen Sie einfach/ruhig.
If you have any questions, please feel free to interrupt.	Sollte es irgendwelche Fragen geben, so fragen Sie einfach.
Feel free to interrupt at any time.	Sie dürfen mich ruhig jederzeit unterbrechen.
If you have any questions, raise your hands!	Wenn Sie Fragen haben, so bitte ich um Handzeichen.

II. 8. Aufforderung zu Fragen

During the lecture	Während des Vortrags
Does anybody have any questions right now?	Gibt es dazu momentan (irgendwelche) Fragen?
Does anybody wish to make a point here?	Möchte irgendjemand etwas dazu anmerken?
Any considerations or comments at this point?	Gibt es bis hierher Überlegungen oder Kommentare?
Do you have any questions at this stage?	Haben Sie Fragen bis hierher?
Any suggestions, ladies and gentlemen?	Vorschläge, meine Damen und Herren?
Before we continue, are there any questions or comments on ...?	Bevor wir fortfahren, gibt es (irgendwelche) Fragen oder Kommentare zu ...?
I'd like to move on (to ...) unless there are any questions.	Ich würde dann gerne (mit ...) fortfahren, es sei denn, es gibt irgendwelche Fragen.
If there are no further questions I'd like to proceed to the next section of my presentation.	Wenn Sie keine weiteren Fragen haben, dann würde ich gerne mit dem nächsten Abschnitt meines Vortrags fortfahren.
Which of you had difficulty following the last topic? Could you please give me a show of hands?	Wer von Ihnen hatte Schwierigkeiten dem letzten Thema zu folgen? Ich bitte um Handzeichen.
Has anyone anything further they wish to add before we move on to the next issue?	Hat jemand noch etwas, das er vorbringen möchte, bevor wir zum nächsten Thema/ Punkt übergehen?

> **INFO:** *Äußerst gebräuchliche Universalkonstruktion um Personen beiderlei Geschlechts anzusprechen; vgl.:* Everybody gets what they deserve

Yes, please!	Ja bitte!
Fire away!	Schießen Sie los!
Go ahead!	Nur zu!

> **INFO:** *Informell, aber durchaus ge-braüchlich, als Reaktion auf eine An-frage aus dem Publikum i. S. v.:* Would you mind if I asked a few questions right now?

At the end of the lecture	Am Ende des Vortrags
Have you got any questions? *(BE)*	Haben Sie Fragen?
Do you have any questions? *(AE; ver-drängt zunehmend die BE-Variante)*	Haben Sie Fragen?
Do you have <u>some</u> questions? *(Diese Va-riante wird oft als höflicher empfunden)*	Haben Sie Fragen?
Have you any questions? *(BE; sehr förm-lich. Auch im AE zu finden)*	Haben Sie Fragen?
Any (more) questions?	Noch Fragen?
Any further comments?	Möchte jemand noch etwas vorbringen? / Weitere Anmerkungen?
Does anybody have any questions?	Hat irgendjemand Fragen?
Doesn't anybody have any questions?	Hat (denn) niemand (mehr) Fragen?
I will take your questions now.	Sie dürfen nun Ihre Fragen an mich rich-ten.
I am now open for your questions and comments.	Ich stehe Ihnen jetzt für Fragen und Kommentare zur Verfügung.

II. 8. Aufforderung zu Fragen

I would like to address any questions you may have now.

Jetzt würde ich gerne auf Ihre Fragen eingehen.

I am happy to take any question now.

Ich beantworte jetzt gerne jede Frage.

I'll be happy to answer any question.

Ich werde gerne jede Frage beantworten.

Are there any other questions?

Gibt es (noch) weitere Fragen?

Are there any more questions?

Gibt es noch Fragen?

Any further questions on this?

(Gibt es) Weitere Fragen hierzu?

Any further points (you wish to raise) before we bring this meeting/session to an end?

(Gibt es) Weitere Punkte(, die Sie ansprechen möchten,) bevor wir die Sitzung schließen?

Anything else? Any more bright thoughts?

Fragen? Anregungen?

I am looking forward to debating these issues with you in just a minute.

Ich freue mich schon, diese Themen gleich mit Ihnen zu diskutieren.

Well, if nobody has any more questions I'd like to thank you all for your attention.

Nun, wenn niemand mehr Fragen hat, dann danke ich Ihnen allen für Ihre Aufmerksamkeit.

9. Antwort auf Fragen, Anmerkungen und Einwände / How to answer and retort

Universals	Neutrale Antwortfloskeln
Thanks for bringing this up.	Danke, dass Sie das sagen.
Thank you for this interesting question.	Danke für diese interessante Frage.
Thank you for your contribution.	Danke für Ihren Beitrag.
This is an excellent question.	Das ist eine sehr gute Frage.
You have just mentioned something very important.	Sie sprechen da etwas sehr Wichtiges an.
You have just raised a very important point.	Sie haben soeben einen sehr wichtigen Punkt angesprochen.
Your question leads us straight back to the subject.	Ihre Frage führt uns unmittelbar zum Thema zurück.

Agreement	Zustimmung
That's true.	Das ist wahr.
That's right.	Das ist richtig.
You are exactly right!	Sie haben genau recht!
You are absolutely right in saying that …	Sie haben absolut recht, wenn Sie sagen, dass …
Good point!	Richtig!
Absolutely!	Absolut (richtig)!
Certainly!	Mit Sicherheit!
Definitely!	Ganz genau!
Exactly!	Exakt!
Spot on!	Den Nagel auf den Kopf getroffen! *(sinngemäß)*

145

II. 9. Antwort auf Fragen, Anmerkungen und Einwände

That about sums it up.	Kann man so sagen.
That's about the size of it.	Richtig.
	Gut zusammengefasst.
I agree with you.	Ich stimme Ihnen zu.
I agree with Dr Smith on that point.	Ich stimme Dr. Smith in dieser Sache zu.
I quite agree with Dr Smith.	Ich stimme Dr. Smith völlig zu.
	(*Anm.: British understatement i. S. v.* That was quite good)
I fully/entirely/totally agree with Dr Smith.	Ich stimme Dr. Smith voll und ganz zu.
I am with Janis on this issue.	In dieser Sache pflichte ich Janis bei.
I am in complete agreement.	Ich stimme dem völlig zu.
Dr Smith is right to bring us up to date.	Es ist gut, dass uns Dr. Smith auf den aktuellen Stand bringt.
As usual, Professor Arkwright is on top of his subject.	Wie gewohnt beherrscht Professor Arkwright sein Fach.
I see absolutely no objection to that.	Ich habe keinerlei Einwände dazu.
I can't put it any better.	Ich kann's nicht besser formulieren.
Believe me; I am not opposed to that.	Glauben Sie mir, ich habe nichts dagegen.
I second your proposal, Mr Chairman.	Herr Vorsitzender, ich unterstütze Ihren Vorschlag.
I'm sure Dr Chelsea will endorse your view.	Ich bin sicher, dass Ihnen Dr. Chelsea zustimmt.
I think we are all agreed on that.	Ich denke, in diesem Punkt stimmen wir alle überein.
I concur with my colleague.	Ich stimme mit meinem Kollegen überein.
I concur on that point.	Ich gehe in diesem Punkt konform.
I am entirely of your opinion.	Ich bin völlig Ihrer Meinung.

II. 9. Antwort auf Fragen, Anmerkungen und Einwände

Your proposal, it seems, has just met with unreserved approval.	Es sieht so aus, als wäre Ihr Vorschlag soeben auf uneingeschränkte Zustimmung gestoßen.
That's a very good point!	Gut, dass Sie das sagen …
	Sehr guter Hinweis!
This is beyond question.	Das steht außer Frage.
I must admit that …	Ich muss zugeben, dass …
I'd rather we hadn't made that mistake, but it's a bit late for that now. I do apologise.	Mir wäre es lieber, wir hätten diesen Fehler nicht begangen, aber es ist wohl zu spät dafür. Ich entschuldige mich aufrichtig.

Restricted agreement	**Eingeschränkte Zustimmung**
You are right, in a way.	In gewisser Hinsicht haben Sie recht.
You are partially right.	Zum Teil haben Sie recht.
You are not completely wrong, but …	Sie haben nicht ganz unrecht, aber …
Could you perhaps be a little more specific?	Geht es vielleicht ein wenig genauer?
I agree with you to a certain extent.	Bis zu einem gewissen Maß stimme ich Ihnen zu.
I can see your point (of view), but I fail to see its relevance.	Ich verstehe Ihren Standpunkt, aber was hat der mit unserer Sache zu tun?
It depends.	Kommt darauf an.
Although it must be admitted that …, there is no denying the fact that …	Zugegebenermaßen …, dennoch lässt sich nicht abstreiten, dass …
Concerning method A, you are right.	Was Methode A anbelangt, haben Sie recht.

II. 9. Antwort auf Fragen, Anmerkungen und Einwände

Disagreement	Widerspruch
You have misunderstood me.	Sie haben mich missverstanden.
I actually wanted to say something else.	Eigentlich wollte ich etwas Anderes sagen.
Perhaps I haven't made myself clear. What I'm trying to say is …	Vielleicht habe ich mich unklar ausgedrückt. Was ich versuche zu sagen, ist …
At the risk of repeating myself, (but) …	Auf die Gefahr hin, mich zu wiederholen, (aber) …
Just to clarify something: …	(Nur) Um etwas klarzustellen: …
I would question this assertion.	Ich würde diese Behauptung infrage stellen.
I'm afraid I'll have to take issue with Dr Braddock (over …).	Ich fürchte, ich muss Dr. Braddock widersprechen (bezüglich …).
I don't agree with you.	Ich bin anderer Meinung.
To be quite honest, I don't agree with you.	Ich will hier ganz ehrlich sein – ich bin anderer Meinung.
I take a different view.	Ich sehe das anders.
Frankly, I take a different view.	Offen gestanden sehe ich das anders.
I'm not of that opinion.	Ich bin nicht dieser Meinung.
I'm afraid I'll have to take issue with you (on that), Dr Doyle.	Leider muss ich Ihnen (in dem Punkt) widersprechen, Dr. Doyle.
This is definitely not the point!	Darum geht es hier überhaupt nicht!
This is simply wrong, since …	Das ist schlichtweg falsch, da …
By no means!	Keineswegs!
Far from it!	Weit gefehlt!

II. 9. Antwort auf Fragen, Anmerkungen und Einwände

Your remarks are wide of the mark, I'm afraid.	Ich fürchte, mit Ihren Bemerkungen liegen Sie (deutlich) daneben.
With (all) due respect, Mr Smith, …	Bei allem Respekt/Ihre Meinung in Ehren, Herr Smith, …
Let me get this straight!	Um das ganz klar zu stellen, …
	Lassen Sie mich in aller Deutlichkeit sagen, dass …
It is my considered opinion that …	Es ist meine fundierte/wohlüberlegte Meinung, dass …
I firmly believe that.	Ich bin fest davon überzeugt.
This is my chief concern.	Dies ist mein Hauptanliegen.
May I finish?	Darf ich ausreden?

Doubts and uncertainties	**Zweifel und Unklarheiten**
I'm not quite sure about …	Ich bin mir nicht so sicher, ob …
I'm still not totally convinced.	Ich bin (immer) noch nicht so ganz überzeugt.
That remains to be seen.	Das bleibt abzuwarten.
That has yet to be proven.	Das muss erst noch bewiesen werden.
This is still under discussion.	Das ist noch nicht geklärt.
We don't know this (for sure).	Das wissen wir nicht (mit Sicherheit).
We are getting into slightly difficult territory here.	Wir bewegen uns hier auf unsicherem Terrain.
This is a very controversial issue.	Dieses Thema ist sehr umstritten.

II. 9. Antwort auf Fragen, Anmerkungen und Einwände

If you have no answer	Wenn Sie keine Antwort wissen
I have no answer to your question at the moment.	Ich kann Ihre Frage im Moment nicht beantworten.
I'd rather not comment on that.	Ich möchte mich dazu lieber nicht äußern.
You have caught me off guard!	Jetzt haben Sie mich (blank) erwischt!
I find myself on unfamiliar territory.	Auf diesem Gebiet bin ich etwas unbewandert.
Mr Smith is a much better person to answer your question.	Herr Smith kann Ihre Frage weit besser beantworten.
This question cannot be answered in a nutshell.	Diese Frage lässt sich nicht mit einem Satz beantworten.
This depends on a whole array of factors.	Das hängt von einer ganzen Reihe von Faktoren ab.
Answering your question would be outside the scope of my presentation.	Die Antwort auf Ihre Frage würde den Rahmen meines Vortrages sprengen.
This is not my area of expertise.	Dies ist nicht mein Fachgebiet.
This would be beyond my experience.	Hierzu kann ich nichts sagen.
That would be outside my sphere of competence.	Dies liegt nicht in meinem Kompetenzbereich.
This is a very difficult question to answer.	Diese Frage ist nicht einfach zu beantworten.
This is actually a rather difficult question.	Diese Frage ist in der Tat schwierig zu beantworten.
This is rather a difficult subject to broach.	Dies ist ein heikles Thema.
At the moment I don't have enough information at my disposal (to sufficiently answer your question).	Mir stehen momentan nicht genügend Informationen zur Verfügung(, um Ihre Frage ausreichend zu beantworten).
Acting on my superior's advice I am not authorised to divulge that information. I'm really sorry.	Auf Anraten meines Vorgesetzten bin ich nicht befugt, diese Information preiszugeben. Tut mir wirklich leid.

II. 9. Antwort auf Fragen, Anmerkungen und Einwände

I'm afraid that's confidential.

Tut mir leid – das ist vertraulich/Verschlusssache.

Let's not waste any more valuable time on this ancillary aspect.

Wir sollten nicht noch mehr kostbare Zeit auf diesen untergeordneten Aspekt verschwenden.

We should leave that for later.

Das sollten wir uns für später aufheben.

I would like to put this question off till later.

Diese Frage würde ich gerne auf später verschieben.

I suggest we defer this matter until …

Ich schlage vor, wir vertagen/verschieben diese Angelegenheit bis …

Can we raise that question again after the break? I should have an answer for you by then.

Können wir diese Frage bis nach der Pause aufheben? Bis dahin sollte ich eine Antwort darauf haben.

Answering this question cuts no ice.

Die Beantwortung dieser Frage fällt nicht ins Gewicht.

What point are you trying to make?

Worauf wollen Sie hinaus?

Where is this leading?

Auf was wollen Sie hinaus?

I'm sorry, but I fail to see your point.

Es tut mir leid, ich weiß nicht, worauf Sie hinaus wollen.

I could ask the same of you.

Dasselbe könnte ich Sie fragen.

Multiple questions	Mehr als eine Frage

The answer to your first question is …

D e Antwort auf Ihre erste Frage lautet …

Let me answer your last question first.

Lassen Sie mich Ihre letzte Frage zuerst beantworten.

Now for your next question.

Nun zu Ihrer nächsten Frage.

Could you please repeat your second question?

Könnten Sie Ihre zweite Frage bitte noch einmal wiederholen?

Shall I answer all the questions? I might as well.

Soll ich all die Fragen beantworten? Warum nicht.

II. 9. Antwort auf Fragen, Anmerkungen und Einwände

As we are rather pressed/pushed for time I shall only answer your second question which, to me, is of particular relevance/significance here.

Da uns die Zeit davon läuft, werde ich nur Ihre zweite Frage beantworten. Diese ist von besonderer Bedeutung, wie ich finde.

10. Fragen und Kommentare anbringen – How to ask and comment

Direct questions	Direkte Fragen
I have a question.	Ich habe eine Frage.
I've got a question. *(BE)*	Ich habe eine Frage.
May I ask (you) a question?	Darf ich (Ihnen) eine Frage stellen?
I would like to ask you whether …	Ich würde Sie gerne fragen, ob …
I would like to know if …	Ich würde gerne wissen, ob … Mich würde interessieren, ob …
I am wondering how you …	Ich frage mich, wie Sie …
It would be interesting to know …	Es wäre interessant zu wissen, …
Two questions still remain.	Zwei Fragen sind noch offen.
There's a question I'd like to ask.	Ich möchte eine Frage stellen. *(betont)*
I do have another question!	Ich habe da schon noch eine Frage! *(betont; diese Form ist angebracht, wenn der Redner davon ausgeht, dass es keine Fragen (mehr) gibt)*
… how shall I put it? … Let me rephrase my question.	… wie soll ich sagen? … Lassen Sie es mich anders formulieren.
I'm afraid I didn't quite follow.	Ich habe Ihnen leider nicht ganz folgen können.

Requests	Aufforderungen
Could you please explain once more how …	Könnten Sie bitte noch einmal erklären, wie …
Would you mind giving another example of …	Könnten Sie ein weiteres Beispiel für … anführen?

II. 10. Fragen und Kommentare anbringen

Could you expand/comment on that?	Könnten Sie das noch weiter ausführen?
Would you like to elaborate on that?	Würden Sie darauf noch näher eingehen?
I was wondering if you could elaborate on that?	Würden Sie darauf noch näher eingehen?
Maybe you could show the previous slide again. I think there is some contradiction in the figures.	Vielleicht könnten Sie das letzte/vorherige Dia noch einmal zeigen. Ich glaube, dass sich die Zahlen widersprechen.
At the risk of sounding offensive, I should very much appreciate if you would answer my question.	Ich möchte Ihnen nicht zu nahe treten, aber ich würde es sehr begrüßen, wenn Sie meine Frage (endlich) beantworten würden.
I'm afraid you've just dodged my question.	Ich fürchte, Sie haben meine Frage nicht beantwortet.
	Tut mir leid, aber Sie sind meiner Frage soeben ausgewichen.
Why can't you give a simple answer to a straight question?	Beantworten Sie diese einfache Frage doch geradeheraus.
A straight/straightforward answer wouldn't go amiss now.	Eine geradlinige Antwort käme jetzt nicht ungelegen.
Please correct me if I'm wrong.	Korrigieren Sie mich bitte, falls ich hier falsch liege.
Can you furnish this information?	Können Sie diese Information liefern?

Comment preceding question	**Frage mit einleitendem Kommentar**
This was indeed a very interesting presentation. However, there is one thing I'd like you to explain.	Das war in der Tat eine sehr interessante Präsentation. Dennoch würde ich Sie bitten, einen Punkt zu erläutern.
I found your lecture quite accomplished. Yet, it has raised a few questions.	Ich fand Ihren Vortrag/Ihre Vorlesung sehr gelungen. Dennoch wirft er/sie einige Fragen auf.

At the beginning of your presentation, you mentioned … Could you please provide more information on how this would fit into Dr Wagner's model?	Zu Beginn Ihrer Präsentation erwähnten Sie … Können Sie uns mehr darüber sagen, wie dies mit Dr. Wagners Modell in Einklang zu bringen ist? *(sinngemäß)*

Interrupting with a question	Den Vortragenden mit einer Frage unterbrechen
Excuse me, may I interrupt you?	Verzeihung, darf ich Sie unterbrechen?
Could you take us through that again, please?	Könnten Sie das bitte noch mal durchspielen?
Sorry for interrupting you. Could you perhaps leave these visuals on the projector?	Entschuldigen Sie, dass ich Sie unterbreche. Könnten Sie vielleicht die grafischen Entwürfe/Elemente auf dem Projektor belassen?
Sorry to break in/to cut in.	Es tut mir leid, dass ich Sie unterbreche.
May I come in at this point?	Darf ich Sie hier kurz unterbrechen?
If you permit, I'd like to mention that …	Wenn Sie gestatten, möchte ich erwähnen, dass …
With your permission, Sir, I'd like to add some information on …	Wenn Sie gestatten, möchte ich einige Informationen über … anfügen.
Excuse me Madam/Sir! Before you proceed, I would like to ask …	Entschuldigen Sie bitte! Bevor Sie fortfahren, würde ich gerne noch fragen …
Excuse me, but before we move on to the next item, I'd like to …	Entschuldigen Sie, aber bevor wir zum nächsten Punkt/Thema kommen, möchte ich gerne …
I'm terribly sorry to interrupt you (there), but just how accurate is this data?	Es tut mir furchtbar leid, wenn ich Sie (da/hier) unterbreche, aber wie exakt sind diese Daten eigentlich?
I do apologize, but this is simply wrong!	Entschuldigen Sie bitte, aber das ist schlichtweg falsch!

II. 10. Fragen und Kommentare anbringen

Comments	Kommentare
I would like to say/add something.	Ich würde gerne etwas vorbringen/ergänzen.
There is something I would like to say.	Ich würde gerne etwas vorbringen *(betont)*
I would like to comment on …	Ich würde gerne zu … etwas sagen.
Permit me to make a few comments on …	Gestatten Sie, dass ich ein paar Anmerkungen zu … mache.
I'd like to come back to what you've said about …	Ich würde gerne auf Ihre Ausführungen über … zurückkommen.
I'd like to return to what Ms Taylor has just said.	Ich würde gerne auf das zurückkommen, was Frau Taylor soeben gesagt hat.
Let me take up again what Mr Smith has mentioned.	Lassen Sie mich nochmals aufgreifen, was Herr Smith gesagt hat.
Coming back to what you said earlier on, I would ask you to go more into detail.	Um auf das zurückzukommen, was Sie zuvor gesagt haben, möchte ich Sie bitten, mehr ins Detail zu gehen.
You gave a very detailed overview of … Yet, there are some crucial aspects that need mentioning/need to be mentioned.	Sie haben (uns) einen sehr detaillierten Überblick über … gegeben. Es sind jedoch noch ein paar entscheidende Punkte zu erwähnen.
Listening to you and the previous speakers, I get the impression that …	Wenn ich Ihnen und den Vorrednern zuhöre, habe ich den Eindruck, dass …
Am I right?	Sehe ich das richtig?
Is this correct?	Stimmt das so?
Please correct me if I'm wrong.	Verbessern Sie mich bitte, wenn ich da falsch liege.

Second-hand information

Informationen aus zweiter Hand

Where did you come by your information?

Wo haben Sie Ihre Informationen her?

How did you come by your information?

Wie sind Sie an Ihre Informationen gekommen?

Digressing from the subject

Abschweifen

Let me digress for a little while.

Lassen Sie mich kurz abschweifen.

At the risk of getting side-tracked here, we should still listen to what Mr Stringer has to say.

Auf die Gefahr hin, dass wir vom Thema abkommen, sollten wir dennoch zuhören, was Herr Stringer zu sagen hat.

Requesting permission

Erlaubnis von oben einholen

Mr Chairman/Mrs Chairwoman, if I may come in here?

Herr Vorsitzender/Frau Vorsitzende, wenn ich hierzu etwas sagen dürfte?

With the Chair's permission, I should be able to shed some light on this matter.

Wenn der/die Vorsitzende erlauben, so sollte ich es wohl schaffen, ein wenig Licht in diese Angelegenheit zu bringen.

Mild warnings

Warnhinweise

If I may have your undivided attention?

Wenn ich um Ihre uneingeschränkte Aufmerksamkeit bitten dürfte.

We must countenance the possibility that somebody might have fiddled the figures.

Wir müssen die Möglichkeit in Betracht ziehen, dass jemand die Zahlen manipuliert hat.

II. 11. Gemischtes & Nützliches

Response to provoking questions	Reaktion auf provokante Fragen
I'm not going to grace this with an answer.	Sie erwarten doch wohl nicht ernsthaft eine Antwort darauf?
I'm not going to dignify that question with an answer.	Diese Frage ist keiner Antwort würdig.
Smart questions are conducive to progress. This one (clearly) isn't.	Clevere Fragen sind dem Fortschritt zuträglich. Diese hier ist es (offenkundig) nicht.

Caution is necessary	Vorsicht ist geboten
This is a delicate matter.	Das ist ein heikles Thema.
This is an issue of great sensitivity.	Das ist eine sensible Angelegenheit.

No rush	Keine Eile
This matter will be dealt with in due course.	Zu gegebener Zeit kümmern wir uns um diese Sache.
We cross that bridge when we come to it.	Alles zu seiner Zeit.

Not responsible	Nicht verantwortlich
The blame cannot be laid at our doorstep. We had better relay that information to …	Man kann uns nicht den schwarzen Peter zuschieben. Wir sollten diese Information lieber … zukommen lassen.
That's not our department.	Hierfür sind wir nicht zuständig.

Getting other people's opinion	Meinungen einholen
And your verdict is?	Was ist Ihr Urteil? Und Ihre Diagnose lautet?
What is your suggested course of action?	Was schlagen Sie vor? Welchen Weg würden Sie einschlagen?

Information	Informationen
Keep me informed of any developments!	Halten Sie mich über alle Entwicklungen auf dem Laufenden!
Keep me posted!	Halten Sie mich auf dem Laufenden!

Mobile phone *(BE)*/Cell phone *(AE)*	Handy
I should very much appreciate if you turned off your (mobile) phones now.	Ich würde es sehr begrüßen, wenn Sie Ihre Handys nun ausschalten würden.
I'd be grateful if you would switch off your mobiles.	Ich wäre Ihnen dankbar, wenn Sie Ihre Handys abschalten (würden).
In case anybody tried to reach me on my mobile this morning, I need to apologise: no connectivity.	Sollte jemand unter Ihnen versucht haben, mich heute Morgen auf dem Handy zu erreichen, so bitte ich um Verzeihung: Kein Netz.
Reception was poor.	Der Empfang war schlecht.
[Phone rings] I really need to take this (call).	[Das Telefon klingelt] Ich muss diesen Anruf entgegennehmen.
	Da muss ich rangehen.

Idioms	Redewendungen
My plate is rather full at the moment.	Ich habe gerade viel um die Ohren.
That's news to me.	Das höre ich zum ersten Mal.

159

App.

Appendices

Appendix 1   Manuskripteinsendung / How to submit

Grundsätzlich haben Sie zwei Möglichkeiten der Manuskripteinsendung: Sie können das Manuskript als Papierausdruck oder aber über die entsprechende Internetseite der wissenschaftlichen Zeitschrift online versenden.
Letzteres wird heutzutage von den meisten Zeitschriften bevorzugt. Der Autor muss sich in der Regel mit Benutzername *(username)* und Passwort *(password)* registrieren. Hierbei wird man Schritt für Schritt durch eine Reihe von Eingabefenstern geführt.
Bei vielen Verlagen ist mit der Registrierung auch eine Abfrage des Manuskriptstatus möglich; häufig erhält der Benutzer Zugriff auf Online-Datenbanken und Kurzfassungen bereits veröffentlichter Artikel.
Details zur Manuskriptvorbereitung und -einsendung sind bei allen gängigen Magazinen auf der Internetseite abrufbar (die Rubriken heißen meist *For authors*, *Author guidelines*, *Preparing your manuscript*, *Submission guidelines*, *How to submit*, *Manuscript submission*, *Submitting your manuscript* etc.). Manche Zeitschriften akzeptieren keine unaufgefordert eingesandten Manuskripte *(no unsolicited material)*.
Verschiedene Redaktionen haben oft sehr unterschiedliche formale Anforderungen an ein Manuskript, weshalb Sie in jedem Falle die spezifischen Anweisungen und Anforderungen für Ihre Manuskripteinsendung beachten müssen. Die nachfolgend aufgeführten Punkte stellen lediglich eine kurze Zusammenfassung wichtiger Kriterien dar.

Im Allgemeinen gilt, dass das Manuskript von Ihnen verfasst sein muss, bisher unveröffentlicht *(previously unpublished)* ist und nicht gleichzeitig an andere Zeitschriften gesandt wurde *(not under consideration for publication elsewhere*; *no simultaneous submissions)*.

Für die Manuskripteinsendung sollten Sie folgende Dinge parat halten:

1. Eine knappe Zusammenfassung Ihres Artikels *(synopsis*; *abstract)*.
2. Den Artikel im geforderten Format.
3. Ein Begleitschreiben (AE: *cover letter*; BE: *covering letter*).
4. Alle weiteren von der Redaktion geforderten Angaben zu *authorship responsibility*, *copyright transfer*, *financial disclosure* etc.
   (Hier sei auf die *submission guidelines* der Zeitschriften verwiesen.)

Zu 1.:
In den *submission guidelines* der Redaktionen finden Sie Angaben zu Inhalten und Umfang des *abstract*. Üblicherweise wird hier eine kurze Beschreibung Ihrer Arbeit sowie der wichtigsten Thesen und Schlussfolgerungen gefordert.

Zu 2.:
Achten Sie auf Vorgaben zum Format: Papierausdrucke *(hard copy)* sollen oft im jeweiligen Landesformat, also z. B. *US letter format* anstatt DIN A4 eingesandt werden. Für elektronische Einsendungen *(electronic submission)* sind nur bestimmte Dateiformate erlaubt (z. B. WORD .doc, .rtf oder .pdf).
Auch hier gelten häufig Beschränkungen hinsichtlich Umfang bzw. Wortzahl.

App. 1   Manuskripteinsendung

Zur Gliederung eines Manuskripts gibt es sehr unterschiedliche Vorgaben. Die folgende Variante stellt eine elementare Struktur für ein wissenschaftliches Manuskript dar. Diese liegt auch dem Aufbau dieses Buches zugrunde.

1. *Introduction*
2. *Materials and methods*
3. *Results*
4. *Discussion/Conclusion*
5. *Acknowledgements*
6. *References*

Je nach Art der Arbeit und redaktionellen Vorgaben sind hier natürlich zahlreiche Variationen möglich.
Sehr oft wird der Abschnitt *Materials and methods* als *Supplementary Information* gar nicht mehr in der Printversion publiziert, sondern nur im Internetauftritt der Zeitschrift.

Zu 3.:
Im *cover letter* sollten folgende Punkte enthalten sein:

- Titel des Manuskripts (*manuscript title*, *title of the paper*)
- Hauptaussage der Arbeit (*statement of the main point*)

Optional sind an dieser Stelle auch noch weitere Aspekte zu berücksichtigen (je nach *submission guidelines*):

- Manuskriptumfang/Wortzahl (*word count*)
- Namentlicher Vorschlag von Personen, die das Manuskript begutachten sollten (*reviewer*)
- Art der Publikation (*type of manuscript*; z. B. *original article*, *review*, *case report* etc.)
- Erwähnung weiterer Publikationen oder Vorträge, die in Bezug zur aktuellen Arbeit stehen.

Einen Sonderfall stellt der *cover letter* für ein überarbeitetes (*revised*) Manuskript dar.
Neben einer Zusammenfassung der vorgenommenen Änderungen am Manuskript sollte hier auf die Empfehlungen der *reviewer* explizit und Punkt für Punkt eingegangen werden.

Nachstehend finden Sie Musteranschreiben, die Ihnen eine Formulierungshilfe für Ihren individuellen *cover letter* bieten. Dabei wird auch auf Besonderheiten für den britischen und amerikanischen Sprachraum eingegangen.

Musteranschreiben für britische Fachzeitschrift

Musterstraße 1
12345 Musterhausen
Germany
e-mail: peter.muster@abc.de

Professor M.C. Smith, MD   17 May 2009
Editor of *JOURNAL NAME*
17 Lake Road
Leeds
GW6 2AH
United Kingdom

Dear Professor Smith[1]

Please find enclosed our manuscript *"Development of gallstone surgery in Germany 1991-2003: Results of a multicentre survey"*.
This retrospective analysis of 45,500 cholecystectomies describes the changes in diagnostic and therapeutic strategies following the introduction of laparoscopic cholecystectomy. Our work investigates the surgical and non-surgical complication rates, reintervention rates and mortality rates of conventional vs. laparoscopic cholecystectomy with special focus on treatment standards in choledocholithiasis. Our data confirm the outstanding role of the minimally-invasive surgical technique and reveal a clear trend towards endoscopic treatment of bile duct stones.
We believe this manuscript to be of interest to many readers of *JOURNAL NAME* and hope it is suitable for publication.

Yours sincerely[2]

Peter Muster, MD

[1] Nach der Anrede steht im BE kein Satzzeichen; allerdings kann ein Komma gesetzt werden. Ist die betreffende Person namentlich bekannt, so setzen Sie z. B. *Dear Professor Smith* und schließen mit *Yours sincerely*. Titel und Anredeformeln *(MD, Ms, Mr, Dr)* werden i. d. R. ohne Abkürzungspunkte angeführt. Sollten Sie keinen namentlichen Adressaten haben, so haben Sie die Auswahl zwischen *Dear Sir(s)* bzw. *Dear Madam* und *Dear Sir or Madam*. In diesen Fällen heißt die Schlussformel *Yours faithfully*. Ist das Schreiben an eine weibliche Person gerichtet, die keinen akademischen Titel trägt und von der Sie nicht wissen, ob sie ledig oder verheiratet ist, so lautet die Anrede z. B. *Ms Taylor* (und nicht *Mrs* oder *Miss*).

[2] Wenn Sie regelmäßig mit einem bestimmten Ansprechpartner kommunizieren, so verwenden Sie ruhig *Best wishes* oder *Best regards/Kind regards* als abschließende Formel – diese setzen sich weltweit immer mehr durch.

Musteranschreiben für amerikanische Fachzeitschrift

Musterstraße 1
12345 Musterhausen
Germany
e-mail: peter.muster@abc.de

Professor M.C. Doyle, M.D.   5/17/09
Editor-in-Chief of *JOURNAL NAME*
110-114 Sunset Boulevard
Suntown, GA 23450
USA

Dear Professor Doyle:[1]

Please find enclosed our manuscript *"Development of gallstone surgery in Germany 1991-2003: Results of a multicenter survey"*.
This retrospective analysis of 45,500 cholecystectomies describes the changes in diagnostic and therapeutic strategies following the introduction of laparoscopic cholecystectomy. Our work investigates the surgical and non-surgical complication rates, reintervention rates and mortality rates of conventional vs. laparoscopic cholecystectomy with special focus on treatment standards in choledocholithiasis. Our data confirm the outstanding role of the minimally-invasive surgical technique and reveal a clear trend towards endoscopic treatment of bile duct stones.
We believe this manuscript to be of interest to many readers of *JOURNAL NAME* and hope it is suitable for publication.

Sincerely[2]

Peter Muster, M.D.

---

[1] Ein Komma anstelle des Doppelpunktes wird als informell angesehen, ist jedoch möglich. Anredekürzel und Titel *(Mr., Ms., Mrs., Dr.)* ziehen im AE immer einen Punkt nach sich. Ist das Schreiben an eine weibliche Person gerichtet, die keinen akademischen Titel trägt und von der Sie nicht wissen, ob sie ledig oder verheiratet ist, so lautet die Anrede z. B. *Ms. Taylor* (und nicht *Mrs.* oder *Miss*). Ist Ihnen der Adressat nicht namentlich bekannt, so verwenden Sie anstelle des britischen *Dear Sirs* die Anrede *Gentlemen*. Als Alternative empfehlen wir das neutrale *Dear Editor(s)*.

[2] Verwenden Sie hier ausschließlich *Sincerely/Sincerely yours/Yours sincerely*.

App. 1   Manuskripteinsendung

Optionale Angaben im *cover letter* können Sie wie folgt formulieren:

- Wenn Sie einen *reviewer* vorschlagen möchten:

  As a potential reviewer we would like to suggest Professor M. Smith (Anschrift, E-Mail, etc.).

- Wenn Sie ein überarbeitetes Manuskript erneut einsenden:

  Please find enclosed the revised version of "Manuscript Title". We have heeded all of the reviewers' propositions (oder Sie nennen die Namen der *reviewer*, wenn dies nicht zu viele sind). *A detailed response to their comments is attached to this letter* (bei *hard copy* Einsendungen)/*is attached as a separate file* (bei einer *electronic submission*).

  Please find enclosed our manuscript "Manuscript Title", which has been revised according to the reviewers' requests …

  Please find enclosed our revised manuscript "Manuscript Title" as requested by the reviewers …

- Wenn Sie eine Eingangsbestätigung wünschen:

  BE: *I/We should be grateful if you would send me/us a brief acknowledgement of receipt.*

  AE: *I/We would appreciate if you sent me/us a brief acknowledgment of receipt.* (Dies erübrigt sich allerdings bei einer *electronic submission*. Darüber hinaus lehnen etliche Redaktionen ein derartiges Verfahren von vornherein ab.)

- Wenn Sie Bezug zu einer Ihrer bisherigen Publikationen herstellen möchten:

  This research paper is based upon the results of one of our former studies as described in "Muster, P. et al., …".

Wenn Sie ein Manuskript per *electronic submission* einreichen, ist Ihnen in der Regel vorgegeben, an welcher Stelle Sie die Inhalte des *cover letter* anbringen. Ein Anschreiben im eigentlichen Sinne ist meist nicht mehr notwendig. Viele Zeitschriften bieten ein eigenes Eingabefenster an, wo Sie aufgefordert werden, entsprechende Informationen unmittelbar einzutragen bzw. einen ausformulierten *cover letter* einzukopieren *(paste)*. Ist dies der Fall, so beginnen Sie den einleitenden Satz nach der Anrede mit *Please find attached* (anstatt *Please find enclosed*).

Einführung

Das heutige Englisch ist geprägt von den beiden großen Varietäten *American English* (AE) und *British English* (BE).

Nachstehend finden Sie die wichtigsten Unterschiede zwischen AE und BE, soweit diese für unser Buch relevant erscheinen. Bei der Orthographie haben wir lediglich einige grundlegende Unterschiede aufgelistet. Jedes gute Textverarbeitungsprogramm verfügt über *spell check* und Spracherkennung, so dass die jeweils gewünschte Varietät des Englischen problemlos eingestellt und das Textdokument automatisch auf Rechtschreibfehler hin überprüft werden kann.

1. Aussprache

Ziel unseres Buches ist es, ein grammatikalisch, idiomatisch, sowie kontextuell und situativ korrektes Standardenglisch im naturwissenschaftlichen Bereich zu vermitteln. Aus diesem Grunde wurde auf Lautschrift und Aussprachevariationen verzichtet. Zudem liegt der Schwerpunkt eindeutig auf der Schriftform. Wenn Sie bei einem englischen Vortrag ein Wort falsch betonen oder fehlerhaft aussprechen, so wird Ihnen das der Muttersprachler sicherlich verzeihen.

Zwei Phänomene sollten Sie dennoch bei der Aussprache intus haben:

Der Buchstabe *z* wird im AE [zi:] gesprochen, im BE [zed].
Wenn Sie im BE Zahlenreihen (beispielsweise eine Telefonnummer) aufsagen, so wird die Null wie der englische Buchstabe *o* gesprochen (also „oh"), im AE hingegen wie die Zahl *zero*. Sowohl Briten als auch Amerikaner verwenden jedoch mitunter die Variante des anderen Muttersprachlers. Gerade bei Telefongesprächen ins Ausland benutzt ein Engländer schon einmal das international eindeutige *zero*. Ein amerikanischer Serienstar las *2804/301* wie folgt im TV vor: "Twenty-eight zero four slash three oh one". Verwenden Sie im Zweifelsfalle ruhig *zero*. Dies wird immer verstanden.

	AE	**BE**
3051	three zero five one	three oh five one

Was Sie noch wissen sollten:
Die Zahl *0.3* wird korrekterweise wie folgt gesprochen: "Nought point three" oder verkürzt "point three". Oft hört man, teilweise von Briten, aber v. a. von Iren und Amerikanern "oh point three". Streng genommen gebietet der wissenschaftliche Gebrauch das für Deutsche ungewohnte *nought*.
Handelt es sich um Temperaturangaben, so wird die Null (AE und BE) "zero" gesprochen: "Below zero/Below zero degrees Celsius".

Die Zahl *510* wird im BE "five hundred and ten" gesprochen. Im AE kann *and* wegfallen: "Five hundred ten".
Oft stolpert man über Datumsangaben. Bsp.: *September 1*. Die einfachste Lösung ist, "September one" zu sagen. Es gibt aber natürlich auch die Variationen "September (the) first/The first of September". *October 13* beispielsweise spricht sich am einfachsten "October thirteen". Man muss dies nicht unnötig komplizieren.

	AE	BE
Vorwahl	area code	dialling code
Postleitzahl	zip code	postcode

Nachstehend finden Sie zunächst die wichtigsten Rechtschreibregeln im Vergleich AE/BE. Auf sprachwissenschaftliche Termini wurde hierbei weitgehend verzichtet. Auf wichtige Unterschiede zwischen AE und BE wird ferner im Buch fortlaufend hingewiesen.

2. Verschiedene Schreibweisen

	AE	BE
Verschiedene Endungen	theater, center	theatre, centre
	honor, color	honour, colour
	defense, offense	defence, offence
	catalog	catalogue
Konsonantendoppelung im BE	traveler, wagon	traveller, waggon
Stummes *e* entfällt oft im AE	acknowledgment, judgment, aging	acknowledgement, judgement, ageing

In Kanada tauchen immer wieder Mischformen bei Verlagen auf, die sich bei einigen Ausdrücken für die amerikanische, bei anderen hingegen für die britische Schreibweise entscheiden (*color* aber *centre*). In vielen Fällen wissen selbst Muttersprachler nicht genau, welches nun die originär britische bzw. amerikanische Schreibweise ist. In Zeitungstexten – gerade auch an Schnittstellen zwischen den beiden großen englischsprachigen Nationen wie in Kanada oder in Irland – geht es bunt drunter und drüber.
Für Ihr eigenes Manuskript sollten Sie sich abhängig vom Adressaten für eine Variante – AE oder BE – entscheiden, und diese konsequent verfolgen.

App. 2   Vergleich AE/BE

Wie sind die folgenden Vergangenheitsformen von Verben einzuordnen?

AE	BE
learned, burned, leaned	learnt, burnt, leant

Bei diesen Beispielen handelt es sich streng genommen nur äußerlich um eine andere Schreibweise; eigentlich geht es hier um regelmäßige Verbformen, welche der Amerikaner bei diesen Verben favorisiert und um unregelmäßige Verbformen, welche der Engländer bevorzugt. Mitunter vermischen sich diese Formen aber auch im AE/BE. Sie sollten lediglich wissen, dass es sie gibt.

Es treten stilistisch unterschiedliche Verbformen auf:

AE	BE
We should have gotten more attention.	We should have got more attention.

Die Form *gotten* wird vornehmlich von Amerikanern verwendet und wird in England eher dem Substandard zugeschrieben.

Ein in beiden Sprachen vorhandener Begriff wird unterschiedlich abgekürzt:

AE + BE	AE (aber gelegentlich auch im BE)	BE
advertisement	ad	advert

Verstanden werden selbstverständlich alle drei Formen von beiden Nationalitäten.

3. Gebrauch des bestimmten Artikels

Der Gebrauch des bestimmten Artikels *the* ist für deutschsprachige Lernende oft schwer nachvollziehbar und folgt nicht immer klaren Regeln. In vortragstechnischer Hinsicht jedoch ist dies häufig reine Sprachkosmetik. Man wird es Ihnen nachsehen, wenn Sie *the* falsch setzen oder aus Unsicherheit einfach weglassen. Bei wissenschaftlichen Fachausdrücken steht allerdings i. d. R. kein *the* (z. B. *Laparoscopic appendectomy has been widely accepted* …).

Bei nachstehenden Beispielen steht im AE stets *the*:

AE	BE
The patient was taken to <u>the</u> hospital.	The patient was taken to hospital.
He went to <u>the</u> university. He studied at <u>the</u> university.	He went to university. He studied at university.

Im BE kann der folgende Satz nur eine Bedeutung haben: *I was in the hospital all afternoon.* „Ich war den ganzen Nachmittag (bei ihr/ihm) im Krankenhaus." *Ich* hat also einen Krankenbesuch gemacht. *I was in hospital all afternoon* hingegen suggeriert, dass *Ich* selbst behandelt wurde.
Wird die Universität näher bezeichnet, so heißt es sowohl im AE wie im BE *He studied at* <u>the</u> University of California.

4. Zeitangaben

	AE	BE
9 Uhr 10	It's ten after nine. It's ten past nine.	It's ten past nine.
9 Uhr 15	It's quarter past nine.	It's a quarter past nine.
9 Uhr 35	It's twenty-five to ten. It's twenty-five of ten. It's twenty-five till ten. It's twenty-five before ten.	It's twenty-five to ten.
9 Uhr 30	It's nine-thirty.	It's half past nine. It's half-nine.

Die Beispiele spiegeln eine gewisse Tendenz oder Präferenz wider. Selbstverständlich wird auch in England *nine-thirty* gebraucht; *It's ten after nine* hört man fast ausnahmslos nur von Amerikanern – natürlich wird sich daran in England niemand stoßen.
Bei dem 9-Uhr-30-Beispiel haben wir Ihnen mit *It's half-nine* eine in den USA gänzlich unbekannte Variante präsentiert; diese ist jedoch in Großbritannien weit verbreitet und auch in Irland sehr dominant. Man darf nur nicht von *half-nine* auf „halb neun" schließen, denn letzteres wäre im BE *half-eight* (also *half past eight*). Die Schreibweise ohne Bindestrich ist ebenfalls gebräuchlich (z. B. bei der Wiedergabe von Dialogen). Da es sich in der Praxis um ein rein gesprochenes Phänomen handelt, sind diese orthographischen Beobachtungen lediglich akademischer Natur. Als Zeitangabe in einem wissenschaftlichen *paper* werden Sie *half-nine* nicht finden. Im Small Talk (Verabredungen etc.) wird es Ihnen häufiger begegnen.

App. 2   Vergleich AE/BE

Das aus dem militärischen Sprachgebrauch herrührende *19:00* oder *19.00* oder *1900* („nineteen hundred (hours)") wird häufig im Managementbereich gebraucht, um Eindeutigkeit zu gewährleisten: *We resume the meeting at nineteen hundred* (*hours*). *Her heart stopped at fifteen oh-five hours (15.05).*

	AE	BE
eine halbe Stunde	a half hour	half an hour

Alternativ können Sie jederzeit *thirty minutes* verwenden.

	AE	BE
zwei Wochen	two weeks	a fortnight two weeks

5. Sprachreinheit

5.1. Vermeidung von nicht sinntragenden Füllwörtern und Interjektionen

Der weit verbreiteten amerikanischen Vorliebe für das redundant gebrauchte Füllwort *like* (auch *kind of*, *sort of*) sollte man entschieden entgegentreten, sonst verfällt man rasch in ein für den Zuhörer anstrengendes und schwerfälliges Argumentieren. Zudem läuft man Gefahr, sich der Lächerlichkeit preiszugeben. Achten Sie doch spaßeshalber bei amerikanischen Talkshows und Nachrichtensendungen auf Phänomene wie dem im Deutschen verankerten *äh* und gewöhnen Sie sich eine entsprechende gegenläufige Sprachdisziplin an. Britische Geschäftspartner werden es Ihnen danken. Als abschreckendes Beispiel sollen die folgenden Sätze dienen:

* He had like a stroke. (Lieber: *He had a stroke* / *He seems to have had a stroke*).
* They are kind of like friends. (Lieber: *They seem to be friends* / *They are indeed friends*).

Bei dem nachstehenden Beispiel sollte man sich mit *rather* bzw. *somewhat* behelfen:

* It's kind of irrational. (Also entweder *It's irrational* oder *It's rather/somewhat irrational*).

Zu erwähnen wäre ebenfalls das stilistisch überflüssige *you know*, welches als Interjektion bei Amerikanern und Briten gleichsam äußerst beliebt scheint, und sich bei Nicht-Muttersprachlern mit einsetzender Müdigkeit und nachlassender Konzentration gerne einschleicht.

* These tests, you know, they are, you know, difficult.

Die Kombination aller drei Tabufloskeln sollten Sie tunlichst vermeiden. In einer, egal wie gearteten Kommunikation, sei es Small Talk oder Business, haben sie nichts verloren.

172

Vermeiden Sie auch modische Kraftausdrücke wie *awesome* (dominant im AE) und *gorgeous* (dominant im BE, v. a. in Irland häufig gebraucht).

5.2. Keine affektierte Hebung der Stimme bei Aussagesätzen

Ein nerviges Sprachphänomen der letzten Jahre trifft v. a. in England auf Unverständnis. Es handelt sich dabei um das Heben der Stimme am Ende gewöhnlicher Aussagesätze, die sich dann wie primitive Fragen anhören. Bei australischen Sprechern ist dies oft sehr ausgeprägt, und auch US-Amerikaner praktizieren dies zum Teil exzessiv. Man spricht hier von *HRT* (*habitual rising terminal*). Dies ist generell zu vermeiden, da sich der Gesprächspartner vermeintlich bevormundet und affektiert behandelt fühlt.

> * *That new product* (?) *The one we read about last week* (?)

5.3. Gebrauch der Inversion

Eine in beiden Sprachräumen auftretende hochsprachige Variante ist die sog. Inversion, also eine Umstellung der Satzbausteine. Sie zeugt von feinem Sprachgefühl und grammatikalischer Korrektheit und wird meist von deutschen Sprechern aus Unsicherheit vermieden. Nehmen Sie doch nachfolgende Beispiele als guten Sprachgebrauch in Ihr Repertoire auf:

> *Under no circumstances will I allow it.*
> *Not only did we succeed in persuading Chinese clinics to participate in the new scheme,*
> *we also managed to sell them the necessary equipment.*
> *At no time were we offered adequate compensation for that loss.*

5.4. Gebrauch des Konjunktivs

Nachstehende Sätze gelten als Standard und sollten in Ihrem Repertoire nicht fehlen:

> *It's high time we went home.* (AE wie BE)
> *It is high time that we went home.* (Förmlicher; AE wie BE)
> *I suggest that Mr Stuart go on with his report.* (AE wie BE)
> *He was insistent that we be present.* (AE-Tendenz – hier recht häufig anzutreffen und nicht als ausgesprochen formell angesehen; diese Konstruktion ist im BE äußerst förmlich und wird fast ausschließlich in stringenter Schriftform, z. B. Gesetzestexte, Dienstanweisungen, Nachrichtenberichterstattung, verwendet)
> *He was insistent that we should be present.* (BE-Tendenz, aber auch im AE zu finden)
> *I suggest that these cases be reviewed with an open mind.* (Interessanterweise favorisieren irische Sprecher i. d. R. diese Variante)

In der Regel steht der Konjunktiv nach Verben wie *order, request, insist, demand, recommend* bzw. nach Konstruktionen wie *it is important/vital/necessary that*:

> *I am going to recommend that Dr Jones undertake ...*
> *Dr Manz has suggested that this meeting be adjourned.*

App. 2   Vergleich AE/BE

Bedeutungsunterscheidender Gebrauch im nachfolgenden Beispiel!

> Forderung: *Dr Soames insisted that we all <u>be</u> present.* (Dr. Soames bestand darauf, dass wir alle anwesend sein sollten.)
>
> Feststellung: *Dr Soames insisted that we all <u>were</u> present.* (Dr. Soames hielt an der Aussage fest, dass wir alle anwesend waren). *Were* ist hier der Indikativ, nicht der Konjunktiv.

Über den diffizilen Gebrauch der Konjunktivformen sind ganze Abhandlungen geschrieben worden. Nehmen Sie einfach zur Kenntnis, dass es ihn gibt und eignen Sie sich einige feste Wendungen an. Ihr anglo-amerikanischer Gesprächspartner wird aufhorchen. Sie bekunden dadurch auch ein tieferschürfendes Interesse an der englischen Sprache.

Abschließend noch zwei nützliche Floskeln:

	AE	**BE**
Mach's gut!	Be good!	Take care!
Es geht mir gut/Ich bin satt.	I'm good.	I'm fine.

Vergessen Sie nie: Sprache ist lebendig und unterliegt ständigem Wandel.

Das nachstehende Wirtschaftsenglischbrevier erhebt naturgemäß keinen Anspruch auf
Vollständigkeit. Vielmehr möchten wir Ihnen Schlüsselbegriffe vermitteln, welche in Ihrem
Arbeitsbereich von Nutzen sein können. Auf Konferenzen und Tagungen kann es durchaus
sein, dass Sie von ausländischen Kollegen in ein Gespräch verwickelt werden, in dessen
Verlauf Sie Ihre Situation/Ihren Arbeitsplatz beschreiben möchten. Wie erklären Sie etwa
einem Engländer, dass Sie unter Personalmangel leiden oder rote Zahlen schreiben?
Hierzu möchten wir Ihnen eine Reihe von Hilfestellungen und Formulierungsmöglichkeiten
anbieten, sowie Ihre Sensibilität für kontextuelles Lernen schärfen. Anhand der Vokabel *to
meet* erkennen Sie, welch vielfältige Kombinationen und Bedeutungsunterschiede in der
englischen Sprache auftreten können. Substantive wie *issue* oder *item* haben gar Dut-
zende von Nuancen. Versuchen Sie daher stets ganze Sinneinheiten zu erlernen. Die
vollständig ausformulierten Beispielsätze vermitteln darüber hinaus auch Besonderheiten
der englischen Grammatik.

allocation	Decisions about the **allocation** of resources are still pending.	Entscheidungen bezüglich der **Zuweisung/Vergabe** von Betriebsmitteln stehen noch aus.
appointment	Can we make/arrange an **appointment** for September 30?	Können wir einen **Termin** für den 30. September vereinbaren?
	Can we still cancel this **appointment**?	Können wir diesen **Termin** noch absagen?
	Can we defer/put off/postpone this **appointment**?	Können wir diesen **Termin** verschieben?
best practice	Dr Merton's model is an innovative example of **best practice**.	Das Modell von Dr. Merton ist ein richtungweisendes Beispiel für **optimales/bewährtes Vorgehen**.
budget	Unfortunately, our **budget** won't run to another consultant *(BE)*/senior physician *(AE)*.	Leider lässt unser **Budget/ Haushalt** keine weitere Oberarztstelle zu.
collective bargaining	I understand (that) **collective bargaining** has reached a deadlock.	Wie ich höre, sind die **Tarifverhandlungen** zum Stillstand gekommen.
fixed-term	I'm still on a **fixed-term** employment contract.	Mein Arbeitsvertrag ist immer noch **befristet**.
flexitime	We have just employed another staff member with **flexitime** arrangements.	Soeben haben wir einen weiteren Mitarbeiter auf **Gleitzeit** eingestellt.

175

fringe benefits/ employee benefits	Does this form of remuneration include **fringe benefits/employee benefits**?	Beinhaltet diese Form der Vergütung **Sozialleistungen**?
glass ceiling	Why don't we discuss the disadvantages of a **glass ceiling** with the aim of abolishing it altogether?	Lassen Sie uns doch die Nachteile einer **Aufstiegsbarriere** diskutieren, mit dem Ziel, diese ganz abzuschaffen.
job creation scheme	I was wondering if we could discuss the financial ins and outs of a new **job creation scheme**.	Könnten wir vielleicht die finanziellen Einzelheiten einer neuen **ABM** (Arbeitsbeschaffungsmaßnahme) besprechen?
leeway	In the USA, flextime workers are given broad **leeway** in setting their own work schedule.	In den USA lässt man dem Personal auf Gleitzeit breiten **Spielraum** bei der Einteilung ihrer Arbeitszeit.
meritocracy	Our modern **meritocracy** continues to raise a host of issues from which health care is not exempt.	Unsere moderne **Leistungsgesellschaft** wirft weiterhin eine Unmenge an Fragen auf, welche auch die medizinische Versorgung betreffen.
time in lieu	I'm afraid adequate **time in lieu** (for overtime) is not an option.	Es tut mir leid, aber angemessener **Freizeitausgleich** (für Überstunden) ist keine Alternative/steht nicht zur Debatte.
income statement *auch*: **profit and loss statement (P&L)**	Last year's **income statement** shows that we are still in the red.	Die **GuV** (Gewinn- und Verlustrechnung) des vergangenen Jahres besagt, dass wir immer noch rote Zahlen schreiben.
profitability	Would you mind explaining what you mean by "**profitability**"?	Würden Sie bitte erklären, was Sie unter „**Rentabilität**" verstehen?
royalties	**Royalties** from SurgeonPublishing&Co. amount to $5,680.	**Tantiemen** von SurgeonPublishing&Co. belaufen sich auf 5.680 Dollar.
scope	There will be no **scope** for investment.	Es wird keinen **Spielraum** für Investitionen geben.
SOP (standard operating procedure)	Unfortunately, we had to deviate from **SOP**.	Leider mussten wir von der **Routinevorgehensweise** abweichen.

state-of-the-art	So far, we have received four different quotations for this **state-of-the-art** device.	Wir haben bislang vier unterschiedliche Preisangebote für dieses **hochmoderne** Gerät erhalten.
	This is **state-of-the-art** technology.	Diese Technologie ist **auf dem neuesten Stand**.
terms of payment and delivery	**Terms of payment and delivery** have yet to be stipulated.	**Zahlungs- und Lieferbedingungen** müssen erst noch vereinbart/festgesetzt werden.
thumbs-up	Our project has been given the **thumbs-up**.	Unser Projekt hat **grünes Licht** (bekommen).
to attend to	I would like to chat with you but Dr Shannon and I have urgent business matters **to attend to**.	Ich würde mich gerne mit Ihnen unterhalten, aber Dr. Shannon und ich müssen uns um dringende geschäftliche Angelegenheiten **kümmern**.
to cut back (on)	How about **cutting back** on temporary work?	Wie wäre es, wenn man bei der Zeitarbeit **einspart/kürzer tritt**?
to cut corners	I suggested that we should **cut corners**, but Charles wouldn't have it!	Ich schlug vor, **Einsparungen vorzunehmen**, aber Charles wollte nichts davon wissen!
	We tried **to cut** (some) **corners** and just encountered more and more problems.	Wir wollten **das Verfahren abkürzen** und stießen dabei auf mehr und mehr Probleme.
to expire	My contract **expires** in May.	Mein Vertrag **läuft** im Mai **aus**.
to extend	My contract has recently been **extended**.	Mein Vertrag wurde kürzlich **verlängert**.
to get onto s.th.	Sarah has promised **to get onto** it asap.	Sarah hat versprochen, sich so bald wie möglich **darum zu kümmern**.
to implement	Three new projects will be **implemented** in the Southern Region of Namibia.	Im südlichen Teil Namibias wird man drei Projekte **umsetzen/verwirklichen/realisieren**.
to meet	~ a deadline	eine Frist **erfüllen/einhalten**
to meet	~ a target	eine Zielvorgabe **erfüllen**
to meet	~ certain requirements	bestimmte Voraussetzungen/Anforderungen **erfüllen/einhalten**
to meet	~ the standard	der Norm **entsprechen**
to meet	~ with approval	auf Zustimmung **treffen**
to meet	~ with success	Erfolg **haben**

App. 3 Ausflug ins Wirtschaftsenglisch

to pull the plug

The **plug** has just been **pulled** on a series of Ukrainian health studies.

Einer Reihe von Gesundheitsstudien in der Ukraine hat man soeben **den Hahn zugedreht**.

to recoup

We must **recoup** our financial losses!

Wir müssen unsere finanziellen Verluste **ausgleichen/wiedergutmachen**.

to streamline

Genesis Pharma has already adopted first-class electronic data capture in order to **streamline** its clinical trials.

Genesis Pharma hat bereits erstklassige EDV eingeführt, um ihre klinischen Studien zu **rationalisieren**.

to summon

This goes no further, John! We will have to **summon** a confidential meeting first thing in the morning.

Das bleibt unter uns, John! Wir müssen gleich morgen früh eine vertrauliche Sitzung **einberufen**.

to the expense of

What we are talking about are accrued debts **to the expense of** €150m.

Wir sprechen hier über aufgelaufene Schulden **in Höhe von** 150 Millionen Euro.

trade union *(BE)/* **labor union** *(AE)*

Our **trade union** *(BE)/***labor union** *(AE)* is going to exact better wages and working conditions.

Unsere **Gewerkschaft** wird mit Nachdruck bessere Löhne und Arbeitsbedingungen fordern/ verlangen.

understaffed

I'm hopelessly **understaffed**.

Ich habe **zu wenig/nicht genug Personal**.

works council

Works councils are arguably necessary to adequately represent the interests of the employees.

Betriebsräte sind wohl notwendig, um die Interessen der Belegschaft angemessen zu vertreten.

Appendix 4 | Kontakte knüpfen / Socialising

Nachstehend finden Sie Floskeln zur Gesprächseröffnung (linke Spalte) und die korrespondierenden möglichen Antworten (rechte Spalte). Wenn Sie den Gesprächspartner bereits kennen, beziehungsweise ein freundschaftliches und eher lockeres Verhältnis zueinander pflegen, dann können Sie problemlos die mit *coll.* (*colloquial*/umgangssprachlich) gekennzeichneten Einträge verwenden. Variationen und Kombinationen sind immer möglich. Nutzen Sie die nächste Tagung doch einfach, um diese Floskeln zu erweitern.

Begrüßung		
How do you do?		How do you do?
Professor Stilton, how do you do?		How do you do?
How are you?		How are you?
	oder	Fine, thanks, how are you?
	oder	I'm fine.
	oder	Not too bad. And yourself?
How are things? *(coll.)*		Fine.
	oder	All right.
How have you been keeping? *(coll.)*		Not too bad.
	oder	(I) Can't complain.
Good to see you again, Nancy!		And you, Thomas!
	oder	Same here.
Delighted to see you again, Dr Carroll.		You haven't changed at all!
	oder	Glad to see you, too.
What a surprise! How are you? It's been a while.		Good to see you again! How are you?
	oder	Nice to see you again. I didn't know you were here.
Long time, no see. *(coll.)*		Right!
	oder	(It) Must have been ages/years.
	oder	I can hardly remember last time we met.
Is it yourself, Sean? *(coll.)* *(In Irland gebräuchliche Wendung für* Good morning*)*		Peter! How's it going?

App. 4   Kontakte knüpfen

Vorstellung		
Have we met before?		Yes, we have.
	oder	I suppose we have.
	oder	I don't think so.
	oder	I don't remember.
	oder	Sorry, I'm not very good with faces.
Hello, I am Peter Anderson from Bristol Central.		Hi Peter, what can I do for you?
Good evening, sir. You may not remember me but we met at the Calgary Conference last year.		Oh, yes, Doctor Miller, I believe? How are you?
Doctor Lawson, I've heard your lecture on … and I would like to introduce myself. My name is Stefan Hollmer.		How do you do?
Good morning. If I may introduce myself? Robert Shelton. I was wondering if you could spare a moment, Professor.		Nice to meet you, Robert. How can I be of service?
Excuse me, Professor Lindgren, have you got a minute? I'm Doctor Schiller from MIT. Would you mind if I asked a straightforward question?		No, not at all, Doctor Schiller. Nice to meet you. Go on.
John, meet my wife Dana.		Hello Dana, pleased to meet you.
	oder	Hello Dana, how are you?
John, I'd like you to meet our new executive secretary, Mrs Diane Kealing.		How do you do?
John, this is Doctor Liane Farrow, our medical director *(BE)*/chief physician *(AE)*		Dr Farrow, I'm pleased to meet you.
Denis, I'd like to introduce my new colleague, Miss Heidi Sandhurst, MD. *(Antwort:)* How do you do?		How do you do?
Larry, may I introduce you to Sally Neville, our principal consultant?		I'm very pleased to meet you.
Sally, meet Phil from Salzburg. Phil, this is Sally, our lab technician.		*(Unzählige Möglichkeiten für S – P, darauf zu reagieren)*

Please allow me to introduce Paul Greatorex from Queen's University.		Nice to meet you, Paul.
(mögl. Antwort:) The pleasure is all mine. Nice to meet you, too.	oder	
		Here's my business card.
(mögl. Antwort:) And here is mine.	oder	
Thank you very much.		

Verabschiedung

(It's been) Nice meeting you, Sally.		Nice meeting you (too), Robert.
It's been a pleasure.		Hope to see you again soon.
	oder	Same here. (Bye now.)
	oder	Take care.
	oder	Looking forward to seeing you again.
Let's keep in touch.		Sure.
	oder	Here's my email. Drop me a line!
I'll be in touch. Good-bye.		Good-bye.
I'll be seeing you one of these days, I hope.		Sure. Take care.
	oder	Great. Bye now.
Listen, I'm off now. Why don't you give us a ring? (coll.)		I will. Have a nice trip.
	oder	Safe journey!
	oder	I'll phone you tomorrow, shall we say at 9 a.m ?
I'm a bit pushed for time. Can I call you later?		Sure, no problem.
	oder	No sweat. (BE coll.)
	oder	Don't worry. It can wait.
	oder	(There's) No rush!
	oder	But of course (you can).

App. 4   Kontakte knüpfen

Will I see you later?		Sure, why not?
	oder	Absolutely!
	oder	By all means.
	oder	I hope so.
	oder	I'll try.
	oder	I've got to pop back to the office but I shan't be long. *(BE)*
	oder	I'm afraid I'll be off soon.
	oder	I won't be here tonight. Sorry.
	oder	Sorry, Paul, I'm taking the seven o'clock flight to Birmingham.
	oder	I'm afraid I'm on the eight o'clock train (back) to Munich.
	oder	I'm sorry, but I'm having prior commitments.
	oder	Sorry, I think I'm going to call it an early night.
What about some coffee?		Good idea, but I'm buying!
Anyone for coffee?		Sounds great.
Shall we grab some tea?		Most definitely.
(In Großbritannien umfasst Tea *am späten Nachmittag oft bereits das Abendbrot, also einen größeren Snack)*		
Why don't we meet at the conference café after the afternoon session?		Sounds good.
	oder	Suits me fine.
	oder	Fine by me.
Any plans for tonight?		Not yet. (Why?)
	oder	Not yet. Why are you asking?
	oder	No. What do you have in mind?
	oder	Not yet. What have you in mind?
Would you like to join me for dinner?		Yes, I would.
	oder	No offence *(BE)*/offense *(AE)* meant but I'd rather stay in tonight.
No offence *(BE)*/offense *(AE)* taken. Another time, perhaps …		

I'm seeing Dr Wolf at eight. We are having dinner at the Savoy. Would you like to come along?		Thank you for asking, I will.
	oder	Don't get this wrong, Harry, but I think I'll be going home straight away after the conference.
Let's go for a pint, shall we?		You're on. *(coll.)*
	oder	OK.
	oder	Great idea!
	oder	I thought you'd never ask!
Fancy a drink?		Sure, why not?
	oder	Let's go!
	oder	Where are we going?
Care for a drink at the bar?		Good idea.
	oder	I do (indeed).
	oder	By all means.
	oder	I wouldn't say no.
My round.	*oder*	
Next round's on me.	*oder*	
I'm buying.		
Can I get you anything?		Sure, I'll have an espresso, please.
	oder	No, thanks, I'm fine *(BE)*/good *(AE)*.

Heutzutage finden sich beide Schreibweisen wie selbstverständlich nebeneinander in der englischen Sprache: *email/e-mail*. Unserer Auffassung nach verdrängt die erste Variante jedoch zunehmend die zweite mit Bindestrich.
Grundsätzlich gilt der wirtschaftliche Grundsatz *KISS* (*keep it short and simple*) auch beim elektronischen Schriftverkehr. Wir möchten Ihnen hier in knapper Form wichtige Eigenheiten von englischen E-Mails vermitteln.

a) *Subject Line* / Betreffzeile

Tragen Sie in jedem Falle etwas ein. Eine *blank subject line*/Leerzeile ist tabu.

Beispiel:

- *Submission on "Pathogenesis and Host Defense"*
- *Abstract*: *Serpins in T cell immunity*
- *Application for Analyst Position Listing 08LAB13*
- *Follow-up to our meeting of Feb 23 at Richmond Tech job fair*

b) *Greetings and Salutations* / Grußformeln und Anrede

Sie wissen nicht, ob der Empfänger ein Mann oder eine Frau ist?
In diesem Falle verwenden Sie die Positionsbezeichnung der betreffenden Person.

Beispiel:

- *Dear Project Manager*
- *Dear Editor*

Alternativ können Sie die Formel *Dear Sir or Madam* verwenden.

Gleiches gilt, wenn Sie eine Gruppe von Personen anschreiben.

Beispiel:

- *Dear Santa Monica Computational Designers*
- *Dear Human Resources Department Staff*

Vor allem in den USA ist es nicht anstößig, wenn Sie die förmliche Anrede unter den Tisch fallen lassen, gerade wenn Sie auf Augenhöhe bzw. in einer höheren Position stehen als der/die von Ihnen Angeschriebene.

Beispiel:

- *Hello – I saw your web site and I would like to mention that …*

Wenn Sie bereits wiederholten Kontakt hatten, so genügt oft ein einfaches *Hi*.

Beispiel:

- *Hi – Are you interested in arranging a meeting for ..*

Die amerikanische Ostküste, ebenso wie Großbritannien, legt im Allgemeinen höheren Wert auf Formalitäten als die Westküste.

Schreiben Sie an John Stilton, so verwenden Sie die Form el *Dear Mr Stilton (BE)* bzw. *Dear Mr. Stilton (AE)* oder *Dr/Dr.* anstelle von *Mr.* Der Vorname wird in Verbindung mit *Mr/Ms/Dr* nicht verwendet. Weibliche Personen, die Sie nicht persönlich kennen, werden mit *Ms (BE)* oder *Ms. (AE)* angesprochen, also *Dear Ms Chalmers.*

Beispielvarianten:

- *Dear Betty Munro*
- *Dear Ms Munro* (BE)
- *Dear Ms. Munro* (AE)
- *Dear Boris Johnson* (BE)
- *Dear Boris T. Johnson* (AE)
- *Dear Sir or Madam*
- *Dear Dr Soames* (BE)
- *Dear Dr. Soames* (AE)

Im Übrigen verweisen wir auf die formellen Restriktionen und Konventionen im Appendix 1.

c) *Reading email addresses* / Aussprache

Gerade wenn Sie am Telefon nähere Angaben zu Kontakten machen möchten, ist es wichtig, dass Sie wissen, wie man E-Mails korrekt angibt.

Beispiele:

- r.coulter@science-blot.co.uk (r dot coulter at science dash blot dot co dot u k)
- hero_doc@sharpmail.ie (hero underline doc at sharpmail dot i e)
- rob_trader@astor.de (rob understroke trader at astor dot d e)
  Underline und *understroke* werden synonym verwendet.

Das deutsche Minus (–) kann im Englischen unterschiedlich wiedergegeben werden. Die universellste Variante ist *dash*. Einige Muttersprachler favorisieren *minus*, da ein *dash* streng genommen zwischen zwei Freizeichen steht, diese aber in einer Webadresse nicht vorhanden sind. Es gibt Amerikaner, die *dash* bevorzugen, aber auch Briten, die diesem Usus folgen. Viele bevorzugen hingegen auf beiden Seiten des Atlantiks das *minus*, aber auch *hyphen* hört man gelegentlich. Ein verbindlicher Konsens ist in der Frage *dash/minus* nicht auszumachen. Nützlich bei der Angabe von Internetseiten sind auch die Zeichen:

/	*forward slash* oder *slash* oder *stroke*
//	*two slashes*
\	*backslash*
:	*colon*
~	*tilde* oder *swung dash.*

App. 5 E-Mails

d) *Acronyms* / Kürzel

Vor allem in den USA werden unzählige Begriffe gerne mit wenigen großen Buchstaben abgekürzt. Im medizinischen Bereich ist dies ebenso überproportional vertreten wie im militärischen. Wir raten im Schriftverkehr zu Zurückhaltung, es sei denn Sie bezeichnen allgemein bekannte Begriffe wie FBI, HTML, JPEG, DNA, ICU. Letzteres bedeutet zum einen *Intensive Care Unit*, kann zum anderen aber auch *I see you* heißen. Im E-Mailverkehr bedenkenlos einsetzbar sind folgende drei Kürzel:

- *BTW (by the way)*
- *FYI (for your information)*
- *TIA (thanks in advance)*

e) *Closing* / Schlussformeln

Verwenden Sie in Ihren E-Mails einfach eine der drei folgenden Alternativen:

- *Best regards*
- *Kind regards*
- *Best wishes*

Schlussbemerkung

- Achten Sie auf eine knackige und aussagekräftige Betreffzeile
- Beginnen Sie mit Ihrem stärksten Argument bzw. Ihrer wichtigsten Idee
- Halten Sie die einzelnen Abschnitte so kurz wie möglich und so lang wie nötig
- Verwenden Sie bei längeren E-Mails Zwischenüberschriften, sog. *sub-topic headings*

Denken Sie an den Dreisatz *write, rest, revise* (Schreiben, Pausieren, Überprüfen).

Appendix 6: Glossar / Glossary

A

Abbildung	figure	42
Abfall	decrease	92, 93
abhängen von	to depend on	84, 85
	to relate to	73, 74
ablehnen: etw. ~	to object to s.th.	80
	to reject s.th.	80
Abnahme	decline	93
abnehmen	to decline	93
	to decrease	60, 93
abschätzen	to estimate	62, 63
abschließend	final	96, 97
	finally	82, 104
	in conclusion	82
	to conclude	82, 104, 105
abschließend betrachtet	in a final analysis	105
absegnen	to endorse	77, 78
Absicht	intent	15
absinken	to decline	93
abweichen (von)	to deviate (from)	71, 72
	to vary (from)	71, 72
Abwesenheit: in ~ von	in the absence of	85
ähnlich	similar	57, 70
aktuell	current	96, 97
Akzent: den ~ setzen (auf)	to focus (on)	54
alle	all (of)	38, 41
alles	all (of)	38, 41

Glossar

alles entscheidend	paramount _____ 55
	vital _____ 55
alles in allem	in summary _____ 104
	in total _____ 39, 41
	on the whole _____ 105
Alter	age _____ 31
Analyse	analysis _____ 17, 18
analysieren	to analyse *(BE)* _____ 26, 27
	to analyze *(AE)* _____ 26, 27
andere(s)	another _____ 50
	other _____ 50
andererseits	on the other hand _____ 56, 58
anders	different _____ 71
anders als	unlike _____ 58
anerkennen	to acknowledge _____ 46, 106, 107
Anerkennung	acknowledgement *(BE)* _____ 106, 107
	acknowledgment *(AE)* _____ 106, 107
anfänglich	initial(ly) _____ 96, 97
anführen	to name _____ 45
angeben: Daten ~	to express data _____ 23
annehmen	to assume _____ 88
	to presume _____ 88
	to suppose _____ 88
Ansicht	view _____ 90
Ansicht: der ~ sein	to suppose _____ 88
Ansicht: der ~ sein, dass ...	to hold the view that ... _____ 90
Ansicht: Unserer ~ nach	In our view _____ 90
ansprechen: etw. ~	to address s.th. _____ 18, 64
ansteigen	to increase _____ 93

Anstieg	gain	93
	increase	92, 93
Anteil	proportion	38, 40
Antwortrate	response rate	22, 23
anwenden: (einen Test) ~	to employ (a test)	28
anzeigen	to indicate	35, 64
Arbeit	work	17, 18
Argument: ein ~ für etw. liefern	to provide an argument for s.th.	77, 78
Artikel	article	17, 18
Assistenz	assistance	106
auch	also	50
aufdecken	to disclose	45, 46
	to reveal	45, 46
auffällig	striking	55
aufgeklärtes Einverständnis	informed consent	32
aufgrund fehlender	in the absence of	85
aufgrund von	because of	73
	due to	73, 74
	owing to	73, 74
auflisten	to list	43
auftreten	to be present	35
	to be seen	35
	to encounter s.th.	34, 35, 45, 46
	to occur	36
Auftreten: das ~	occurrence	36
aufwerfen: Bedenken bezüglich etw. ~	to raise concern about s.th.	81
aufwerfen: Fragen über etw. ~	to raise questions about s.th.	81
aufwerfen: Zweifel an etw. ~	to raise doubts about s.th.	81
Aufzählungspunkt	bullet point	42

Glossar

aufzeichnen	to monitor	24
	to record	24
aufzeigen	to indicate	43
Augenhöhe: auf ~ mit … sein	to be on a par with	58
Ausdruck: jmdm. gegenüber Dankbarkeit zum ~ bringen	to express gratitude to s.o.	107
Ausdruck: seinen Dank gegenüber jmdm. zum ~ bringen	to record one's gratitude to s.o.	107
auseinandersetzen: sich mit etw. besonders ~	to focus on s.th.	99
ausgehen: davon ~	to suppose	88
Ausmaß (von)	extent (of)	94
Ausnahme (von)	exemption (from)	33
ausreichende Beweise	ample evidence	78
ausschließen	to exclude	29
Ausschluss	exclusion	29
Ausschlusskriterium	exclusion criterion	29
außerdem	also	50
	besides	49, 50
	furthermore	49
	in addition	49, 50
	moreover	49
auswählen	to select	30
Auswahlkriterien	recruitment criteria	30
Auswirkung (auf)	effect (on)	87
Auswirkung: (erhebliche) ~ (auf)	impact (on)	87
Auswirkung: (geringe) ~ (auf)	bearing (on)	87

B

Balkendiagramm	bar chart	44
Bandbreite	gamut	34, 36
	scale	34, 36
basieren auf	to be based on	84
beabsichtigen	to aim	15
	to be intended to	16
	to set out to	16
beachten	to note	54
beantworten: eine Frage (eindeutig/endgültig) ~	to settle a question	20
bedenken	to acknowledge	46
	to consider	46
Bedenken bezüglich etw. aufwerfen	to raise concern about s.th.	81
bedeutend	significant	55
Bedeutung: von gleichrangiger ~ sein	to be on a par with	58
bedingen	to contribute to	75
bedingt sein durch	to relate to	73, 74
beeindruckend	impressive	55
beeinflussen	to affect	84, 87
	to influence	84, 87
befassen: sich mit etw. ~	to concern oneself with s.th.	19
befassen: sich mit etw. besonders ~	to focus on s.th.	99
Befragte(r)	respondent	22, 23
befürworten	to advocate	77, 78
	to approve of s.th.	79
	to endorse	77, 78
	to favor (AE) s.th.	79
	to favour (BE) s.th.	79
befürworten: etw. nicht ~	to disapprove of s.th.	80
begegnen: etw. ~	to come across s.th.	35
	to encounter s.th.	34, 35, 45, 46

191

Glossar

begleitet werden von	to be accompanied by	85
begründet durch	caused by	73
begrüßen	to approve of s.th.	79
behaupten	to assert	90
	to claim	64, 90
	to contend	90
	to maintain	90
Beilage	supplementary information	22, 24
Beispiel	example	51
Beispiel: zum ~	e.g.	51
	for example	51
	for instance	51
Beistand	assistance	106
beitragen zu	to contribute to	75
bekannt machen	to disclose	45, 46
bekräftigen	to confirm	77, 78
	to corroborate	77, 78
Belang	concern	19
belaufen: sich ~ auf	to stand at	36
bemerken	to mention	45
	to perceive	45, 46
bemerkenswert	remarkable	53, 54
	striking	55
bemerkenswert sein	to be worth mentioning	55
Bemessung	assessment	27
beobachten	to monitor	24
	to observe	34, 35, 45
	to see	35
berechnen	to calculate	26, 27
Bericht	report	17, 18

berichten	to report _____	**45, 46, 64**
Berücksichtigung: unter ~ von	with respect to _____	**84, 86**
beschreiben	to describe _____	**18, 47, 64**
besondere(-n/-s)	special _____	**55**
besonders	particular _____	**53, 54**
	particularly _____	**54**
	special _____	**55**
bestätigen	to confirm _____	**70, 77, 78**
	to prove _____	**77, 78**
bestimmen	to determine _____	**19, 26, 27**
betonen	to emphasize _____	**53**
	to stress _____	**53**
	to underscore _____	**54**
Betracht: in ~ ziehen	to take into account _____	**46**
	to take into consideration _____	**46**
betrachten: etw. genauer ~	to take a closer look at s.th. _____	**98, 99**
betrachtet: abschließend ~	in a final analysis _____	**105**
beträchtlich	considerable _____	**53, 54, 94**
beurteilen	to assess _____	**19, 26, 27, 62**
	to evaluate _____	**19, 26, 27, 62**
beurteilen: etw. auf etw. hin ~	to assess s.th. for s.th. _____	**62**
Beurteilung	assessment _____	**27**
beweisen	to prove _____	**77, 78**
bewerten	to assess _____	**19, 26, 27, 62**
	to evaluate _____	**19, 26, 27, 62, 64**
Bewertung	assessment _____	**62**
beziehungsweise	respectively _____	**37**
Bezug zu	bearing (on) _____	**87**
bezüglich	pertaining to _____	**86**

Glossar

bezuschussen	to fund _____ **106, 108**
	to subsidize _____ **108**
bieten: Unterstützung ~	to provide support for s.th. _____ **77, 78**
billigen	to give one's approval to _____ **79**
	to lend countenance to _____ **79**
bis jetzt	so far _____ **96**
	thus far _____ **97**
bisher	to date _____ **96, 97**
bislang	to date _____ **96, 97**
bringen: (mühsam) in Erfahrung ~	to glean s.th. _____ **25**
bringen: etw. mit sich ~	to be associated with _____ **84**
Bruchteil	fraction _____ **38, 40**

D

d. h.	i.e. *(auch: ie)* _____ **51, 52**
Dank an jmdn. richten	to address thanks to s.o. _____ **107**
	to extend thanks to s.o. _____ **107**
Dank gebührt jmdm.	thanks are due to s.o. _____ **107**
Dank: jmdm. ~ schulden	to owe gratitude to s.o. _____ **107**
Dank: jmdm. zu ~ verpflichtet sein	to be indebted to s.o. for s.th. _____ **108**
Dank: seinen ~ gegenüber jmdm. zum Ausdruck bringen	to record one's gratitude to s.o. _____ **107**
dankbar sein	to be grateful _____ **106, 107**
Dankbarkeit: jmdm. gegenüber ~ zum Ausdruck bringen	to express gratitude to s.o. _____ **107**
danken: jmdm. ~	to address thanks to s.o. _____ **107**
	to extend thanks to s.o. _____ **107**
	to thank s.o. _____ **106**
Danksagung	acknowledgements *(BE)* _____ **106, 107**
	acknowledgments *(AE)* _____ **106, 107**
dann	then _____ **49**
darbieten	to give _____ **43**

darlegen	to report	43
darstellen	to depict	47
	to represent	36
darstellen: plakativ ~	to delineate	47
darüber hinaus	besides	49, 50
	furthermore	49
	in addition	49, 50
	moreover	49
darum	that is (the reason) why …	76
Daten	data	22
Daten angeben	to express data	23
Daten: über etw. ~ erheben	to collect data about s.th.	25
davon ausgehen	to suppose	88
decken: sich ~ mit	to be congruent with	57
definieren (als)	to define (as)	31
demonstrieren	to demonstrate	43, 64, 77, 78
dennoch	nevertheless	59
	nonetheless	59
	still	59
	yet	56, 59
deshalb	hence	75
	therefore	75
deswegen	hence	75, 82, 83
	that is (the reason) why …	76
	therefore	75, 82, 83
	thus	82, 83
Detail: ein unbedeutendes ~	a minute detail	99
Detail: ein winziges ~	a minute detail	99
Detail: ins ~ gehen	to go into detail	98

Glossar

detailliert	detailed	98
	in detail	98
Diagramm	chart	42, 43
	diagram	42, 43
	graph	42, 44
differenzieren (zwischen)	to differentiate (between)	56, 58
dokumentieren	to report	64
Drittel: ein ~ von	one third of	38, 40
Drittens ...	third, ...	49
durchführen	to conduct	17
	to perform	17, 27, 28
durchführen: eine Studie ~	to conduct a study	17
	to perform a study	17
durchführen: einen Test ~	to carry out a test	27
	to perform a test	27

E

einbeziehen: mit ~	to take into account	46
Einblick in etw. gewähren	to offer insight into s.th.	20
eindeutig	clear	75
einerseits	on the one hand	56, 58
Einfluss (auf)	effect (on)	87
Einfluss: (starker) ~ (auf)	impact (on)	87
eingehend	exhaustive	98, 99
einige	a few	38, 39
einnehmen: eine unterschiedliche Haltung ~	to take a different view (on)	71
einreichen	to submit	23
einschätzen	to assess	19, 26, 27, 62
	to evaluate	19, 26, 27, 62

einschließen	to comprise	30
	to enlist	30
	to enrol	30
	to include	29
Einschluss	inclusion	29
Einschlusskriterium	inclusion criterion	29
einstufen (als)	to classify (as)	31
einteilen: in Kategorien ~	to group	30
einverstanden: nicht ~ sein (mit)	to disagree (with)	80
Ende: am ~	in conclusion	104, 105
endgültig	final	96, 97
entdecken	to detect	35, 45, 46
entgegen	contrary to	58
entscheidend	critical	55
	crucial	55
entsprechen	to be equal to	57
	to be the equivalent of	57
	to correspond with	69
	to represent	36
Entwicklung	development	60
erachten: etw. für etw. ~	to believe s.th. to be s.th.	63
	to consider s.th. (to be) s.th.	63
	to deem s.th. (as) s.th. (sehr förmlich)	63
	to regard s.th. as s.th.	63
Erfahrung: (mühsam) in ~ bringen	to glean s.th.	25
Erfahrung: Nach unserer ~ …	In our experience …	91
erfordern	to require	33
erforschen	to explore	19
erforschen: (genauestens) ~	to scrutinize	99
erfragen	to query	23

Glossar

Ergebnis	finding	34
	outcome	34, 35
	result	34
Ergebnis: im ~	as a result	83
Ergebnis: zu einem ~ kommen	to find	34, 35
erhalten: etw. ~	to obtain s.th.	25
erheben: über etw. Daten ~	to collect data about s.th.	25
Erhebung	survey	17
erhöhen um	to increase by	60
erklären	to explain	75
erklären: sich ~ (durch)	to be explained (by)	75
Erklärung	explanation	75
erlangen: über etw. Kenntnis ~	to gain knowledge of s.th.	25
erläutern: etw. detailliert ~	to detail (s.th.)	98
erläutern: etw. genauer ~	to detail (s.th.)	98
erniedrigen um	to decrease by	60
erschöpfend	exhaustive	98, 99
Erstens ...	first, ...	49
	firstly, ...	49
	first off, ...	49
erstere(s)	the former	50
erstmalig	for the first time	21
erwägen	to consider	46
Erwägung: in ~ ziehen	to take into account	46
	to take into consideration	46
erwähnen	to mention	45
	to report	45, 46
erwähnen: jmdn. dankend ~	to show appreciation to s.o.	107
Essay	essay	17, 18

essenziell	essential	55
Ethikkommission	ethics committee	32, 33

F

Fachaufsatz	essay	17, 18
favorisieren	to favor *(AE)* s.th.	79
	to favour *(BE)* s.th.	79
feststellen	to detect	35, 45, 46
	to determine	19
	to find	64
	to identify	35
	to observe	45
	to reveal	35, 45, 46
finden	to find	34, 35, 64
Flussdiagramm	flow chart	43
folglich	as a consequence	73, 74, 82, 83
	consequently	83
	in conclusion	82
	thus	82, 83
Follow-Up	follow-up	22, 24
fördern	to enhance	61
Forschung	research	17, 19
fortführen	to continue	61
Frage: eine ~ (eindeutig/endgültig) beant-worten	to settle a question	20
Frage: etw. in ~ stellen	to challenge s.th.	81
	to question s.th.	81
Fragebogen	questionnaire	22, 23
Fragen über etw. aufwerfen	to raise questions about s.th.	81
Freistellung (von)	exemption (from)	33
früher	previous	96

Glossar

Funktion		
	graph	42, 44
für etw. sein	to be in favor *(AE)* of s.th.	79
	to be in favour *(BE)* of s.th.	79

G

gegen etw. sein	to be against s.th.	80
Gegensatz: im ~ zu	contrary to	58
	in contrast to	71, 72
	opposed to	56, 58
Gegenstand	subject	29
Gegenteil: im ~	on the contrary	56, 58
gegenteilig	contradictory	58, 71, 72
gegenüberstehen: einem Problem ~	to face a problem	100
gegenüberstellen	to contrast	56, 58
gegenwärtig	current	96, 97
	present	96, 97
gering	minor	92
geringfügig	marginal(ly)	93
	slight	93
	slightly	93
gesamt	total	39, 41
Gesamt…	overall	39, 41
Gesamtheit	overall	31
	total	31, 39, 41
Gesamtzahl	overall	31
	total	31
gewähren: Einblick in etw. ~	to offer insight into s.th.	20
gewinnen: etw. ~	to obtain s.th.	25
gewinnen: über etw. Informationen ~	to gather information about s.th.	25

glauben	to believe	91
gleich	identical	57
gleichbedeutend sein	to be the equivalent of	57
gleichzeitig mit	in tandem with	85
Grad	degree	95
gravierend	crucial	55
Grenzen: an ~ stoßen	to encounter limitations	100
groß	vast	94
größtenteils	for the most part	94
	largely	92, 94
Grund: auf ~ von	on account of	76
Grund: aus diesem ~	for this reason	75
	that is (the reason) why ...	76
gründlich	thorough	98
gründlich: (äußerst) ~	meticulous	98
Gruppe	group	31
gruppieren	to group	30
gutheißen	to endorse	33, 77, 78

H

Hälfte: die ~ von	half of	38, 40
halten: etw. für etw. ~	to believe s.th. to be s.th.	63
	to consider s.th. (to be) s.th.	63
	to deem s.th. (as) s.th.	63
	to regard s.th. as s.th.	63
Haltung: eine unterschiedliche ~ einnehmen	to take a different view (on)	71
Hand: auf der ~ liegend	evident	75
häufig	frequent	92, 93
	frequently	93

Glossar

Häufigkeit	frequency _____ 34, 36, 93
	rate _____ 34, 36
Haupt...	main _____ 92, 94
	major _____ 92
Hauptaugenmerk	focus _____ 15, 16
hauptsächlich	main _____ 92, 94
	mainly _____ 92, 94
	major _____ 92
hegen: Zweifel an etw. ~	to harbor *(AE)* doubts about s.th. _____ 81
	to harbour *(BE)* doubts about s.th. _____ 81
heranziehen	to retrieve _____ 24
herausfinden	to find _____ 34, 35
	to glean s.th. _____ 25
herausragend	paramount _____ 55
herrühren von	to originate from _____ 73, 74
	to stem from _____ 73, 74
hervorheben	to foreground _____ 53
	to highlight _____ 43, 53, 54
hervorstechend	striking _____ 55
Hilfe	help _____ 106
Hinblick: im ~ auf	with regard to _____ 84, 86
	with respect to _____ 84, 86
hindeuten: darauf ~	to indicate _____ 35
hingegen	however _____ 56, 59
Hinsicht: in dieser ~	in this respect _____ 86
hinsichtlich	concerning _____ 86
	in respect of _____ 86

Glossar

hinweisen (auf)	to indicate _____	**35, 53, 64, 77, 83**
	to point out _____	**53**
hoch	high _____	**38, 39**

I

identisch	identical _____	**57**
illustrieren	to illustrate _____	**18, 47**
Individuen	individuals _____	**29, 31**
Informationen: über etw. ~ gewinnen	to gather information about s.th. _____	**25**
Informations-Beilage	supplementary information _____	**22, 24**
inhärent	inherent _____	**100**
innewohnend	inherent _____	**100**
insbesondere	in particular _____	**54**
insgesamt	in total _____	**31**
	overall _____	**31, 39, 41, 104**
intensiv	intensive _____	**98, 99**
interessante Fragestellung	question of interest _____	**19**
Inzidenz	incidence _____	**34, 36**

J

jedoch	however _____	**56, 59**

K

Kategorien: in ~ einteilen	to group _____	**30**
Kenntnis: über etw. ~ erlangen	to gain knowledge of s.th. _____	**25**
Kenntnis: zur ~ nehmen	to note _____	**53, 54**
klar	clear _____	**75**
klassifizieren	to classify (as) _____	**31**
Kohorte	cohort _____	**29, 30**
kommen: zu einem Ergebnis ~	to find _____	**34, 35**

Glossar

komplett	total	39, 41
konfrontiert werden: mit einem Problem ~	to be faced with a problem	101
konkordant mit	concordant with	69, 70
konzentrieren: sich (auf etw.) ~	to focus (on s.th.)	53, 54, 99
korrelieren mit	to correlate with	69
Kreisdiagramm	pie chart	44
kritisieren	to criticize	80
Kurve	graph	42, 44
kürzlich	recent	96

L

lebenswichtig	vital	55
letztere(s)	the latter	50
Letztlich …	finally	49, 50
liefern	to provide	23
liefern: ein Argument für etw. ~	to provide an argument for s.th.	77, 78
limitiert sein (durch)	to be limited (by)	100
Limitierung	limitation	100
Lupe: unter die ~ nehmen	to scrutinize	47, 48

M

Mal: zum ersten ~	for the first time	21
manche	some	38, 39
Mangel	shortcoming	101
Manko	drawback	101
marginal	marginal	93
	marginally	93
maximieren	to maximize	95
mehr	more	92
Mehrheit	majority	38, 40

Meinung		opinion _____ 90
Meinung: anderer ~ sein	to	disagree (with) _____ 71, 72
Meinung: Unserer ~ nach		In our opinion _____ 90
messen	to	measure _____ 24
Methode		method _____ 22, 24
Minderheit		minority _____ 38, 40
mindern um	to	decrease by _____ 60
minimieren	to	minimize _____ 95
missbilligen: etw. ~	to	disapprove of s.th. _____ 80
Missstand		drawback _____ 101
multifaktoriell		multifactorial _____ 75

N

nachbeobachten: etw. ~	to	follow s.th. up _____ 24
Nachbeobachtung		follow-up _____ 22, 24
Nachweis von etw.		evidence of s.th. _____ 36
natürlich		inherent _____ 100
neben		besides _____ 50
nehmen: unter die Lupe ~	to	scrutinize _____ 47, 48
nehmen: zur Kenntnis ~	to	note _____ 53, 54
nennen	to	name _____ 45
neu		new _____ 21
neuartig		novel _____ 21
nichts		none (of) _____ 39, 41
niedrig		low _____ 38, 39
niemand		none (of) _____ 39, 41
notieren	to	note _____ 53

Glossar

O

offensichtlich	apparent _____ 74
	evident _____ 75
	obvious _____ 75
ohne	in the absence of _____ 85

P

paar: ein ~	a few _____ 38, 39
parallel	in tandem with _____ 85
Patientenauswahl	patient selection _____ 30
Patientenkollektiv	patient population _____ 29
Patientenpopulation	patient population _____ 29
Person	subject _____ 29, 31
plakativ darstellen	to delineate _____ 47
präsentieren	to present _____ 18, 43
Priorität	priority _____ 16
Problem	problem _____ 100
Problem: einem ~ gegenüberstehen	to face a problem _____ 100
Problem: mit einem ~ konfrontiert werden	to be faced with a problem _____ 101
Prozentsatz	percentage _____ 38, 40
prozentualer Anteil	percentage _____ 38, 40
prüfen	to test _____ 19

R

randomisiert zuteilen	to randomise *(BE)* _____ 31
	to randomize *(AE)* _____ 31
Rat	advice _____ 106, 107
Rate	rate _____ 34, 36, 38, 40
Reduktion	decrease _____ 92, 93
reichen: von ... bis ... ~	to range from ... to ... _____ 34, 36, 95

Reihe	series	29, 30
Reihe (von Probanden)	cohort	29, 30
Reihe: eine ~ (von)	a number of	38, 39
	a score of	38, 39
rekrutieren	to enlist	30
	to enrol	30
	to recruit	30
Resultat	result	34
resultieren aus	to result from	73
richten: Dank an jmdn. ~	to address thanks to s.o.	107
	to extend thanks to s.o.	107
Rücklaufquote	rate of return	22, 23

S

schätzen	to estimate	62, 63, 88, 89
Schätzung	estimate	63
Schaubild	chart	42, 43
	graph	42, 44
schildern	to delineate	47
schließlich	finally	49, 50, 82, 104
	in conclusion	104, 105
Schluss	finding	34
schlussfolgern	to conclude	65, 82, 104, 105
Schlussfolgerung	conclusion	82
Schuld: bei jmdm. in der ~ stehen	to be indebted to s.o. for s.th.	108
schulden: jmdm. Dank ~	to owe gratitude to s.o.	107
Schwachpunkt	shortcoming	101
schwanken: von ... bis ... ~	to vary from ... to...	95
Schwankungsbreite	variation	95
Schwerpunkt	focus	15, 16

Glossar

Deutsch	Englisch	Seite
Schwerpunkt: den ~ setzen bei	to focus (on)	53
schwerwiegend	major	92
sein: für etw. ~	to be in favor *(AE)* of s.th.	79
	to be in favour *(BE)* of s.th.	79
sein: gegen etw. ~	to be against s.th.	80
selten	rare	92, 93
	rarely	93
Serie	series	29, 30
setzen: den Akzent ~ (auf)	to focus (on)	54
signifikant	significant	26, 55
Signifikanz	significance	26
sinken	to decline	93
somit	in conclusion	82
sorgfältig: (äußerst) ~	meticulous	98
Spektrum	gamut	34, 36
	scale	34, 36
sporadisch	rare	92, 93
	rarely	93
steigern	to enhance	61
	to increase	93
steigern um	to increase by	60
Steigerung	increase	92, 93
stellen: etw. in Frage ~	to challenge s.th.	81
	to question s.th.	81
stellen: zur Verfügung ~	to submit	23
Stichprobe	sample	29
Stichpunkt	bullet point	42
stoßen: an Grenzen ~	to encounter limitations	100
stoßen: auf etw. ~	to come across s.th.	35

Streudiagramm	scatter plot	44
Studie	study	17
Studie: eine ~ durchführen	to conduct (a study)	17
	to perform (a study)	17
Studienprotokoll	study protocol	22, 23

T

Tabelle	chart	42, 43
	table	42
Teil	part	38, 40
Teil: zu einem großen ~	in large part	94
Teil: zum größten ~	for the most part	94
teilnehmen: (an etw.) ~	to participate (in s.th.)	30
	to take part (in s.th.)	30
teilweise	partial(ly)	38, 40
Tendenz	tendency	60
Test: einen ~ anwenden	to employ a test	28
Test: einen ~ durchführen	to carry out a test	27
Test: einen ~ verwenden	to use a test	27
testen	to test	19, 26, 27
Thema	subject	29
tiefschürfend	thorough	98
Tortendiagramm	pie chart	44
tragend	critical	55
Tragweite	extent (of)	94
treffen: eine Unterscheidung ~ (zwischen)	to make a distinction (between)	58
trotz	despite	59
	in spite of	59

Glossar

trotzdem	nevertheless	59
	nonetheless	59
	still	59

U

Überblick	survey	17
Überblick: einen ~ geben über etw.	to review s.th.	18
übereinstimmen mit	to be congruent with	57
	to be consistent with	69
	to tally with	57
übereinstimmend mit	concordant with	69, 70
Übereinstimmung: in ~ mit	in accordance with	69
	in agreement with	69
	in keeping with	69, 70
	in line with	69, 70
überschätzen	to overestimate	62, 88, 89
Übersicht	survey	17
Übersichtsarbeit	review	17, 18
übersteigen	to exceed	95
übertreffen	to exceed	95
überwiegend	largely	92, 94
	vast	94
überzeugt sein(, dass …)	to be convinced (that)	90
überzeugt sein: (von etw.) ~	to be convinced (of s.th.)	90
Überzeugung: Meiner festen ~ nach …	It is my contention that …	91
um zu	in order to	16
umfassend	extensive	98, 99
unabhängig von	independent of	85
und zuletzt	finally	82

ungeachtet	regardless of	86
Untergruppe	subgroup	31
untermauern	to corroborate	77, 78
unterschätzen	to underestimate	62, 88, 89
unterscheiden (zwischen)	to distinguish (between)	56, 58
unterscheiden: sich ~ von	to differ from	71
Unterscheidung: eine ~ treffen (zwischen)	to make a distinction (between)	58
unterschiedlich	different	71
unterstreichen	to underline	53, 54
	to underscore	54
unterstützen	to lend countenance to	79
	to support	77, 78, 106, 108
unterstützen: (finanziell) ~	to fund	106, 108
Unterstützung	assistance	106
	support	106
Unterstützung bieten	to provide support for s.th.	77, 78
untersuchen	to examine	18, 26, 28, 64
	to explore	19
	to investigate	18, 64
	to study	64
untersuchen: (genauestens) ~	to scrutinize	99
untersuchen: auf etw. hin ~	to screen (for)	24
untersuchen: bezüglich etw. ~	to screen (for)	24
Untersuchung	investigation	17, 19
Untersuchung: eine eingehende ~	a closer examination	99

V

Variabilität	variability	95
	variation	95
variieren: von ... bis ... ~	to vary from ... to ...	34, 37, 95
veranschaulichen	to illustrate	18

Glossar

verantwortlich (für)	responsible (for)	75
verarbeiten	to process	28
verbessern	to enhance	61
verbessern: (sich) ~	to improve	60, 61
Verbindung: in ~ mit	in conjunction with	85
verdeutlichen	to highlight	43
	to illustrate	47
	to specify	47, 48
verfechten	to contend	90
verfügbar	available	23
Verfügung: zur ~ stellen	to submit	23
vergangen	past	96
Vergangenheit	past	96
Vergleich: im ~ (dazu)	in comparison	57
vergleichbar	comparable	57, 70
vergleichbar: etw. ist gut mit etw. ~	s.th. compares favorably *(AE)* with s.th.	70
	s.th. compares favourably *(BE)* with s.th.	70
vergleichen (mit)	to compare (with)	20, 26, 28, 44, 56, 65
Vergleichsarbeit	comparison study	65
Vergleichsstudie	comparison study	65
Verhältnis	proportion	38, 40
vermuten	to assume	88
	to presume	88
	to suggest	88
vermuten lassen	to suggest	88
Vermutung	assumption	88
verschärfen	to exacerbate	61
verschlechtern	to aggravate	61
	to exacerbate	61
verschlechtern: (sich) ~	to deteriorate	60, 61

verstärken	to enhance	61
versuchen	to attempt	16
verursacht von	caused by	73
verursacht werden durch	to be related to	84
verwenden: (einen Test) ~	to use (a test)	27
verzeichnen	to cite	64
	to note	64
	to record	24
verzichten: auf etw. ~	to waive	33
viele	many	38, 39
Vielfalt	variability	95
Viertel: ein ~ von	one quarter of	38
vor allem	above all	53, 54
vorbringen	to suggest	64
vorhergehend	previous	96
vorliegend	present	96, 97
Vorrang	priority	16
vorstellen	to present	18
vorwiegend	predominantly	94

W

wahrnehmen	to perceive	45, 46
was etw. angeht	as far as s.th. is concerned	87
	as for s.th.	84, 85
	in terms of	86
wegen	because of	73
	due to	73, 74
	on account of	76
	owing to	73, 74

Glossar

weitere(s)	another	50
	other	50
weiterlaufen	to continue	61
weitreichend	extensive	94, 98, 99
wenig	little	38, 39
wenige	few	38, 39
weniger	less	92
Wertschätzung ausdrücken	to show appreciation to s.o.	107
wesentlich	essential	55
wichtig	important	53, 55
widerlegen: etw. ~	to disprove s.th.	80, 81
widerspiegeln	to reflect	44
widersprechen	to contradict	71, 72
widersprechen: etw. ~	to object to s.th.	80
widersprechend	contradictory	53, 71, 72
Widerspruch: im ~ zu	in contrast to	58
wie etwa	like	51
	such as	51, 52
wie z. B.	like	51
	such as	51, 52
wogegen	whereas	59
würdigen	to acknowledge	106, 107

Z

zeigen	to demonstrate	43, 64, 77, 78
	to give	43
	to indicate	83
	to present	43
	to show	42, 64, 77
zeigen: sich ~	to reveal	35

Zeitraum	period	22, 24
ziehen: in Betracht ~	to take into account	46
	to take into consideration	46
ziehen: in Erwägung ~	to take into account	46
	to take into consideration	46
Ziel	aim	15
	goal	15
	objective	15
Zielgruppe	target group	16
zu vernachlässigen	marginal	93
	marginally	93
Zugewinn	gain	93
Zukunft	future	96, 97
zukünftig	future	96, 97
zunächst	to begin with	49
zunehmen	to increase	60
zurückführen auf	to attribute to	73, 74
zurückweisen: etw. ~	to reject s.th.	80
zurückzuführen auf	attributable to	73, 74
zusammen	in total	39, 41
zusammen mit	along with	85
	coupled with	85
	in conjunction with	85
	together with	85
zusammenfassen	to summarize	44, 104
	to sum up	104
zusammenfassend	summing up	104
	to sum up	104
zusammenfügen	to combine	44

Glossar

zusammengefasst	in summary	104
Zusammenhang	context	84, 86
zusammenhängen: mit etw. ~	to be associated with	84
	to be related to	84
	to relate to	73, 74
zusammensetzen: sich ~ aus	to consist of	30
zusammenwirken	to combine (to)	75
zustimmen	to approve	32
	to endorse	33
	to give one's approval to	79
zustimmen: nicht ~	to disagree (with)	71, 72
Zustimmung	approval	32, 33
zuteilen: randomisiert ~	to randomise *(BE)*	31
	to randomize *(AE)*	31
Zweck	purpose	15, 16
Zweifel an etw. aufwerfen	to raise doubts about s.th.	81
Zweifel an etw. hegen	to harbor *(AE)* doubts about s.th.	81
	to harbour *(BE)* doubts about s.th.	81
Zweitens ...	second, ...	49